I WANT TO SHOW YOU MY NAME

Right the Wrongs

Mary F. Cook

I WANT TO SHOW YOU MY NAME
Right the Wrongs
All Rights Reserved.
Copyright © 2020 Mary F. Cook
v5.0

The opinions expressed in this manuscript are solely the opinions of the author and do not represent the opinions or thoughts of the publisher. The author has represented and warranted full ownership and/or legal right to publish all the materials in this book.

This book may not be reproduced, transmitted, or stored in whole or in part by any means, including graphic, electronic, or mechanical without the express written consent of the publisher except in the case of brief quotations embodied in critical articles and reviews.

ISBN: 978-0-578-22573-9

Cover Photo © 2020 Mary F. Cook. All rights reserved - used with permission.

Published by MFCook Print

DEDICATION

I dedicate this book to every individual or group of people who has been afflicted by injustice.

May your enemies bow down before you and atone for their sins that they inflicted upon you and all others who were affected by INJUSTICE.

Remember to pray, put God first, and wait on the Lord for guidance and answers to everything on your journey in life.

May God's Miraculous Bright Light of Swift Justice shine on each of you with BLESSINGS BEYOND MEASURE!

May each of you be blessed with longevity and enjoy the fruits of SWIFT JUSTICE that God bestows upon you.

Table of Contents

Special Thanks For My Five Special Friends vii
Preface xi
Acknowledgments xiii

1. GOING HOME/THE WARNING 1
   Billy C and Carrie Frances 1997 2
   I Am Scared of This House 3
   Liniment Cake 5
   Cousin Caleb's Surprise 9

2. GOSSIPING/MEMORY LANE 11
   Caesar's Haircut 13
   Caesar is Hitched Out 14
   Bufus Jumps the Fence 16

3. LIVINGSTON GETS ARRESTED.......................20
   Billy C 32
   Dream Sequence 33

4. REVELATION OF DREAM/BILLY C IS DEAD 37
   Carrie Frances Runs Off/
   I Don't Want To Get Married 38
   Ghost Stories (Hant-Hank) 43
   Hardware Store 45
   Coming Clean with Benjy 48
   Paying Respect/Gathering Info 50

5. FIREPOWER 53
   Palmetto Motel Resort 54
   The Unholy Five/Reunion/Flashbacks 55
   Verlie's Flashback-1973 56
   Baby Doll's Flashback-New York-1976 58
   Teri's Flashback-New York-1975 61
   Tracy Flashback-1974-Brooklyn N.Y. 66
   Carrie Frances Flashback-Sept. 1974 76

6. OLD COUNTRY STORE WITH
   CONFEDERATE FLAG 82
   Patti Cake Flashback-Nov. 1975 84

7. A LOT'S GOING ON TODAY 91
   Good Old Times Again 92
   Saying Goodbye 93
   Burn, Baby, Burn 94
   Destiny 96
   At Last 102

8. NEW YEAR'S EVE CELEBRATION 105
   John The Baptist 108
   9 Encounters Identical Twins Lookalike 110
   Bible Thief 118
   Flashback-1973 New York City 118
   The Real Story Statler Hilton Hotel 118
   Statler Hilton Hotel-Different Room-
   Another Day 119
   Statler Hilton Hotel-Different Room-
   Another Day 119
   Abraham And Straus-December 1973 120
   Carrie Frances's Apartment-1973 120
   The Funeral 122
   Shears Church Cemetery 124
   Happy New Year 125

EPILOGUE 126

SPECIAL THANKS FOR MY FIVE SPECIAL FRIENDS

To Shellie, thank you for being my prayer partner.

To Halerie, thank you for all of your kindness over the years.

To Ronald, thank you for being there for me and understanding when I need you most.

To Bernard, thank you for being a brother to me for all of these years.

TO THAT SPECIAL PERSON: I thank God for letting the two of us be at the right place and time, on that BEAUTIFUL SPRING EVENING, when our HEARTS and SOULS met and experienced the meaning of TRUE LOVE. MY HEART and SOUL were yours from that moment until now and will continue to be yours forever. I also know that YOUR HEART and SOUL will be mine forever as well.

When God puts two hearts and souls together as he did ours, NO MAN, WOMAN, NOR CHILD will be able to break that

LOVE. If, by chance, we should travel different paths, our hearts and souls will love each other through eternity.

BUT, if it's GOD'S WILL that he BESTOWS his MERCIFUL, GRACIOUS, EVERLASTING ONE LOVE upon us, then our HEARTS AND SOULS will be as ONE LOVE, SANCTIFIED LOVE.

IN MEMORY OF
Ms. Alice Spears

Ms. Sister Spears-Hagan

Mr. Toot Hagan

Asper Spears

Luvenia McLaughlin-Spears

Rose McLaughlin

Nathaniel McLaughlin

Ms. Lou Hailey

Mrs. Deeley McRae

Ms. Mattie Watters

Henry Watters

Catherine Cook

Mildred Cook

Advert Woods

Steven Bishop

Werner Sherer

Sally Mae Cook-Benn

Alberta Cook-McCrae

Willie B. David

Charles (Al) Stewart

PREFACE
By
Mary F. Cook

I Want to Show You My Name is a fact-based story with a slight twist of fiction; names and places have been changed to protect the innocent. It is a story about love and friendship between friends and the depths that they would go to protect one another. What starts out as a sweet, anticipated Christmas holiday vacation, with hopes of rekindling an old love relationship, turns into a nightmare for the main character, Carrie Frances. So, on New Year's Day, instead of going to the movies with her high school sweetheart as she had hoped for, she was attending his funeral. Shortly after hearing of his death, she was in a REVENGE and JUSTICE mood. She not only got justice for her sweetheart but for everyone else she felt had an INJUSTICE done to them in the past—especially for one old lady who was unjustly mistreated over fifty years prior. To get this justice, she had to reach back into her well-hidden past. By doing this, it made it easier for Carrie Frances to deal with the loss of her beloved childhood sweetheart; and it brought her great joy and gratification to get justice for the old lady. It also strengthened the bond of loyalty, love, and friendship with her longtime friends, for whom at times in the past she had been a SAVIOR.

ACKNOWLEDGMENTS

I give the praise, thanks, and the glory to God, my heavenly Father. Without You, I wouldn't be here. Thank You for my life. Thank You for giving me such loving, caring, wonderful, and God-fearing parents, who raised me to believe in You from a very young age. I've called on You daily from my childhood. You have always answered, and I will continue to put my total trust in You as long as I live.

I thank my parents for teaching me the values of good morals in life. Thank you for giving me the choice to use my God-given "individualized mind" that was bestowed upon me at birth. Now that I have acknowledged all of the above, I can get on to the ones who inspired this book.

Every story has characters; every character has a story. If the characters didn't have a story worth telling, then there would not be a story. Now, hear this, no matter who the person (character) is, there is a story;

whether it's boring or exciting, someone is interested in their story. Having said that, I want to acknowledge the following people who made Carrie Frances's story possible and brought it to life in this book.

My childhood friend, **Ola Lea McClendon-McNeil,** thank you for keeping me grounded and updated about the happenings around town. You are indeed my sister by another mother, even though we grew up together since we were babies. I love you.

Cherry Annette Crookes, my dear friend I met right out of high school. It was a blessing to meet you. Everyone needs a best friend. I love you and miss you so much. Because of you, Cherry, I met some of the other characters in this book. I thank you for that because some of them brought great joy to my life. And most importantly, you made it possible for me to have an encounter with so many of my HOMIES! Writing this brings tears of joy to my eyes and happiness in my heart. May God's blessings be upon you and your family always (your children and Loris and her children, Bonnie and Darrel).

Wynn Crown, thank you for wanting a can of beer and not being able to afford one.

Daniel Crown, thank you for being such a great negotiator and knowing a great deal when you hear and see one.

June Bug Crown, thank you for asking that question and when I answered, you and Daniel laughed.

Well, look who I met after that.

Bunny Crown, I'll always remember the night we met. Oh, what a night! Thanks, Daniel and June Bug, another HOMIE.

Till Noody, when I walked into a certain club that night and saw you, I couldn't believe my eyes. I was so happy and then you said, "Gerry Zan is downstairs." I couldn't believe what I was hearing; I was beyond HAPPY.

Gerry Zan, when I saw you and Till, it was like I was home hanging out at one of the clubs, but here we were, in BROOKLYN. The two of you were a sight for sore eyes.

Necola Mensch, you were the first one I saw sitting at the bar as I entered the club. I knew then that Daniel and June Bug were right. I saw people I honestly had not seen since I was a small child, but I knew their faces.

Moffee Bones, thank you for looking out for me as a big brother.

Keri Hams, thank you for being such a great friend. I really enjoyed our fun times together.

Baby Doll, thank you for knowing when to "fold" and when to "hold." You did good for yourself, and I am very proud of you, and I love you.

Pattie Cake, thank you for being a great friend and knowing when to take sound advice. It pays off. I love you and I am extremely, very proud of you!

Francie Callen, I don't know where to begin with

you. I will never forget the day that I met you and little Lane. That was the beginning of a lifetime friendship. The things that you and I have seen and endured and yet, we are still standing strong. I am so happy and proud of the life that you have made for yourself. May God's blessings be upon you and your children, Lane and Vikki, always. I love you, my friend.

I acknowledge all of you and MAY GOD'S BLESSINGS OF HEALTH, PROSPERITY, HAPPINESS, PEACE, SUCCESS, and LOVE BE UPON ALL OF YOU FOREVER!

1

GOING HOME/
THE WARNING

New York City, Friday, December 20, 2002, 4:45 AM. A limousine pulls up to the curb. A beautiful, well-built, stylishly dressed, fortyish brown complexion, African American woman gets out on the passenger side. As she gets out of the car, a gunshot is heard within her mind and she smiles.

She gets her luggage and walks to the curbside check-in. Suddenly she hears a voice from within saying, "Watch out for your luggage." She goes through the checkpoint and walks to the gate. She boards the plane, finds her seat, and sits down. She opens her purse, takes out an invitation to a premiere, and smiles. On the invitation you see her name, "Carrie Frances." As she is looking at the invitation, she smiles and says to herself, "I am going to show you my name." Carrie Frances, still smiling and holding the invitation, has flashbacks of her beloved high school sweetheart.

Billy C and Carrie Frances 1997

Carrie Frances and Billy C, a handsome, fair skinned, young fiftyish African American man, are sitting in the living room looking at photographs and magazines from the theatre. Billy C says to her, "I am so proud of you. If you had stayed and married me, we would have had a good life, but you would not have traveled to all of these places, seen and done all of this great work." He looks at Carrie Frances and continues saying, "I forgive you for leaving me." Carrie Frances looks at him and says, "I never stopped loving you, and I never gave my heart to anyone other than you. I still have my daddy's name." (End of Flashback)

Two hours later, Carrie Frances walks to the U.S. Air Terminal in Charlotte, North Carolina. As she enters the waiting area, she sees an empty seat away from the window. She hears a voice from within. That same voice she heard earlier, but this time it is firm and softly saying, "Watch out for your luggage." She sits near the window after hearing that voice and looks for her luggage as the airport workers load the small plane. Immediately, she sees a man putting her luggage on the plane. Momentarily, the man comes off the plane with her luggage and takes it to a nearby plane. The man comes off the plane without her luggage.

Carrie Frances immediately points this out to the man behind the counter and says, "Excuse me, sir, is this plane going to Fayetteville, North Carolina?" The man replies, "Yes, it is." Carrie Frances tells him very confidently, "Well, sir, I know my luggage very well. I just saw a man take my luggage onto the Fayetteville plane and immediately afterward, he took my luggage and put it on another plane. Please go and get my luggage and put it back on the Fayetteville plane." The man replies, "I am going right now."

Carrie Frances looks on as the man puts her luggage back onto the Fayetteville plane. The man comes back over to Carrie Frances and says, "Miss, it was a good thing that you were looking out for your luggage." She smiles and says, "Yes, I know. And by the way, where is that plane going?" The man replies, "Greenville, South Carolina."

I Am Scared of This House

A short time later, Carrie Frances is driving on Highway 95 South passing Palmetto's Motel Resort. Finally, she pulls into her driveway. She enters the house with a scared look on her face. Cobwebs are everywhere. Ladybugs have taken over the house. She runs out of the house and calls her cousin from her cell phone. She tells her, "Mae Evelyn, I am scared to go into my house. There are spiderwebs everywhere and the ladybugs have taken over. There might be snakes in there too. I am scared. What am I going to do?" Her cousin, Mae Evelyn, isn't concerned in the least bit about what is in Carrie Frances' house. She says, "Call your cousin Caleb." Carrie Frances tells her that she doesn't have his number. Then she thinks for a second and says, "I'll drive over to his house and I'll call you back later."

Carrie Frances hurries over to Cousin Caleb's house. When she pulls into his yard, she is met by his five dogs and their puppies running about. Cousin Caleb's house is a run-down house with junk all around it. Car seats are used for porch chairs, and the porch doesn't have a roof on it. Carrie Frances honks the horn. Cousin Caleb comes out to the car. He is very happy to see her.

Cousin Caleb is a fortyish brown-skinned man with a Jeri curl and raggedy teeth. He is smiling and speaks with a tied tongue and says, "Cusin Ker Francie, it's gued to shee you. Chez iis." Carrie Frances, smiling, answers, "It's so good to see you too. I am so glad that you are home today. I need your help. Caleb, you know I haven't been home since Momma died and that was a year-and-a-half ago. I am scared to go into my house. There might be snakes in there. Could you please come with me and help me clean up the place? I'll pay you." He replies, "Yeah, Cusin Ker Francie, I'll go wit you and hep you creen ebeyting."

Shortly afterward, Carrie Frances is sitting at the kitchen table, talking on the phone. You can see the beauty of the house now that Cousin Caleb has cleaned most of it. This is Carrie Frances's ritual. Every time she visits, she spends most of her time sitting at the kitchen table talking on the phone with her best friend Viola; gossiping about the old and new. Carrie Frances, on the phone with Viola, says, "Viola, my house was so dusty, I was scared to come inside. The ladybugs had moved in. I got my cousin Caleb McLaurin to come and clean for me. He's not afraid of snakes. He's cleaning the bedroom now. No telling what's in those closets."

Viola has never left the country; and has a deep country voice. Carrie Frances likes that. By talking to her friends, it keeps her grounded. It also reminds her of her humble beginnings. Viola says, "That's good he came to clean for you. He's real nice anyway. Where does Caleb live?" Carrie Frances says, "He lives down there on the other side of Bufus and Ilene's house. You know, right where Miss Tru Cailey used to live when we were little. You remember, I told you about the old lady that made the liniment cake when I was little." Laughing, Viola says, "I don't remember that. We used to talk about so much stuff. Tell me about the cake." She replies, "Well, one day Miss Calice Shields came through the yard with her adopted granddaughter Marie Rosalina. We all called her Soot. Soot was the age of my sister Mandolyn." Carrie Frances tells Viola the story from flashbacks of her childhood memories.

Liniment Cake

Carrie Frances and her sister Mandolyn are playing in the yard. Mrs. Flora, their mother, at forty-three years old, is a beautiful brown-skinned woman sitting on the front porch. Mrs. Flora says, "Yonder come Miss Calice and Soot. I wonder where she's going today. I guess she's going to Mrs. Baby Sis's house."

Miss Calice is about Miss Tru's age, one hundred plus years, with gray-yellowish hair wrapped in tobacco twine. Miss Calice is wearing a long dress with an apron. She walks with a carved walking stick and has a hoe across her shoulder. She walks into the yard and speaks to Mrs. Flora. Miss Calice is a snuff dipper as well as Mrs. Flora. Miss Calice spits and says, "Hey, Flo." Mrs. Flora smiles and answers, "Hi, Miss Calice.

How you doing? Where you off to this morning? Mrs. Baby Sis?" Miss Calice spits again and says, "Nope, not really. I'm taking Marie Rosalina to see Mattie Kay, Tru's great-gran, and I'm guine to pick some huckleberries. Would you like your younglings to come and play with Mattie Kay?"

Carrie Frances and Mandolyn beg their mother to let them go. Finally, Mrs. Flora gives in to them and says, "All right, you can go, but be on your best behavior." Carrie Frances and Mandolyn follow Miss Calice and Soot. Carrie Frances walk close to Miss Calice, looking at her with admiration. Soot and Mandolyn play together, laughing and giggling. They all jump the ditch and go on to Miss Tru's house, which is an old faded red shack. Mattie Kay is in the yard playing. She and Carrie Frances are around the same age. She has been in the sun so much that her complexion has a deep brown tan with a reddish tone. Her hair is sunburned so bad that it is red also, and it is styled in an old hairdo from Miss Tru's heyday. When she looks up and sees Miss Calice coming down the road, she excitedly yells, "Momma, Miss Calice comin."

Miss Tru appears on the porch looking from underneath her wire-rim glasses. You can see that her glasses are dirty from fingerprints. She takes off her glasses to see Miss Calice. Ms. Tru dresses the same way as Miss Calice does from the 1800s. She is so happy that company is coming that she begins talking to Miss Calice before she enters the yard. Miss Tru Cailey yells, "Calice, you come to see me. Hee-hee, I am so glad you come." She looks at Mattie Kay and says, "Mattie, you got company. That's Soot and Wallace and Flora chilums." She looks at Miss Calice and tells her, "You jest in time. I am making a sweetbread." Miss Calice answers her as she approaches the yard also. Carrie Frances keeps up with every step that Miss Calice makes. Miss Calice replies, "Tru, I'm guine leave the younglings here to play with Mattie Kay while I go and pick huckleberries so you and I can make us a cobbler." Miss Tru says, "All right." Miss Calice doesn't stop for a second; she continues on walking as if she's on a mission. Miss Tru goes back into the house.

The children start playing in the yard, and the sun is shining so bright and beautifully. Suddenly, Mandolyn says, "I smell liniment." Soot answers, "Me too." Mattie Kay says, "Momma rubs with linamy for rumatissium." Then, Carrie Frances says, "My momma rubs her shoulders for rumitissum too." A little while later, Miss Tru appears on the porch and says, "Chilum, come on and get your sweetbread." After a few minutes all of the children are squinting their eyes and frowning but continues eating the sweetbread.

A few hours later Miss Calice brings Mandolyn and Carrie Frances back to their house and continues on to her house with little Soot in tow. Mrs. Flora asks the children about their day at Miss Tru's house. Mrs. Flora asks, "You children had a good time?" Smells and sniffs and says, "You all smell like liniment."

Mandolyn says, "Momma, Miss Tru sent you some sweetbread." Carrie Frances says, "Momma, it don't taste like your cake. It tastes like linamy." Mrs. Flora smells the sweetbread and says, "Poor Miss Tru. She can't see good. She thought she was putting flavor and poured liniment instead. I hope she has enough liniment left over for her rheumatism." (End of Flashback.)

Viola is laughing on the other end of the telephone so hard that she can barely talk. She asks Carrie Frances, "Did you get sick?" Carrie Frances replies, laughing, "No! Momma gave us lots of milk to drink. She made a cake for Miss Tru and took it to her. A few months later, Miss Tru's granddaughter came and got her and Mattie Kay and took them back to New York with her."

Serious and excited, she continues, "I didn't see them anymore until a few years later. I must have been about seven or eight years old. There was a funeral at our church one Sunday. It was in the summertime and I was sitting in the church with lots of other little children." She pauses and continues. "You remember how all the little kids that knew each other would sit together." Laughing, Viola says, "Yeah, I remember that. We would sit and sneak and eat cookies." Carrie Frances laughingly says, "Well, the family hadn't come in yet, and all of a sudden Miss Tru and little Mattie Kay walked in. Everybody in the church got really quiet, stood up, and looked at Miss Tru and Mattie Kay. I stood up too." She pauses and says, "I was so glad to see Miss Tru and Mattie Kay. None of us had seen Miss Tru and Mattie Kay since they left, shortly after Miss Tru made that liniment cake." She thinks for a second and says, "Viola, everybody stood up out of respect for Miss Tru because she was so old. Viola, even then as young as I was, I got goose bumps. I admired Miss Tru so much. She looked so nice; even little Mattie

Kay looked nice too. Viola, you know, you might have been to that funeral too. You know everybody went to funerals, especially on Sundays." Viola says, "I don't remember, but I probably was there. We went to all the funerals. Knowing me, I was probably eating cookies; that's all I did besides looking at the people to see who was going to out-cry the other." Carrie Frances continues, "Well, the last I heard, Mattie Kay got married and was taking care of Miss Tru." Carrie Frances has a far-off look and is nodding her head and says, "Yeah, Miss Tru lived to be about a hundred and fifteen years old, and Miss Calice Shields did too." Then there is a pause, and she looks around. Cousin Caleb is standing behind her and she says, "Viola, I'll call you back. Caleb is finished cleaning. I have to take him home and then go to Walmart. I'll call you when I get back."

Cousin Caleb's Surprise

Carrie Frances and Cousin Caleb comes out of Walmart with four filled shopping carts. Cousin Caleb puts the bags in the trunk and backseat of the car. They drive off and stop by a fast-food restaurant. They are enjoying themselves. It has been a few years since they have seen each other. Caleb gives Carrie Frances all of the gossip. He knows everything that goes on in the town.

When they arrive at Cousin Caleb's house, he gets out of the car carrying a bag of fast food. As he walks toward his house Carrie Frances rolls down the car window and yells to him, "Caleb, you forgot something." Caleb's wife, Cat, a fortyish dark-skinned woman with raggedy teeth comes out onto the porch. Caleb hears Carrie Frances call out to him and looks back with a surprised look and says, "Whut, Cusin Ker Francie?" Carrie Frances, smiling, says, "You forgot all of the things in the trunk that I bought from Walmart." She pops open the trunk. Cousin Caleb, grinning, says, "Cusin Ker Francie, you bought that for me?" Caleb walks back to the trunk. Overjoyed he says, "Cusin Ker Francie, you so gued to me. Cat, come yook, shee whut Cusin Ker Francie bought us." She runs out to the car, looks in the trunk, and helps Caleb carry the bags to the porch. Cat, grinning, says, "Santa Claus come early." Carrie Frances replies, "That's right, Merry Christmas. Caleb, I'll pick you up tomorrow to help me clean Momma's and Daddy's grave." He smiles and says, "I'll be ready and waitin', Cusin Ker Francie." Carrie Frances backs the car up and drives off.

2

GOSSIPING/ MEMORY LANE

Carrie Frances is back at her house now. She has plenty of food from the supermarket. Her house is clean, and she is ready to find out all of the gossip. There is nothing else to do in a small town like this. This is the normal routine on her visits. If she didn't have real estate properties here, she would probably visit about once every five years. She likes to be very comfortable when she is getting all of the news. That's why she cleans first, shops for food second, and then sits at the kitchen table and talks on the phone to Viola until the wee hours of the morning.

She listens to her messages on the answering machine, while digging into a bag of fast food. Viola is very anxious to tell her the gossip. That's why she has already called and left a message on the answering machine instead of waiting for Carrie Frances to call her back after she finished shopping. Viola looks forward to her visits, even though they talk a lot by phone when

Carrie Frances is in New York. Carrie Frances is so anxious to find out the happenings that she calls Viola while eating some French fries. In a happy voice she says, "Viola, it's me, Carrie Frances. I just got back. I took Caleb to Walmart and played Santa Claus to him." Laughing she says, "He didn't know I bought all of those things for him until I dropped him off at home." Viola replies, "Child, I know he was happy." She says, "He sure was, he and his wife." Laughing, Carrie Frances continues, "Viola, his wife's teeth are messed up worse than his." Viola laughs and says, "Carrie Frances, stop laughing at your cousin. I got plenty of gossip to tell you. Where do you want me to start?" She says, "Tell me about Billy C. Is he dating anyone?" Viola tells her, "No, not that I know of. You know how he is. If he is seeing somebody, he's keeping it quiet." Carrie Frances says, "Good, I am going to ask him to take me to see this movie that I did. It's coming out on Christmas Day. I want to show him my name." Viola asks, "What you mean?" She explains, "When we work, we get screen credits." Viola says, "Oh, I see, he'll enjoy that." Carrie Frances says, "Yeah, some years ago, I showed him all of my work from the Broadway Theater and he was very happy. He said he was so proud of me. That was when he told me that he forgave me for running off and leaving him. Viola, I feel so bad for running off that night."

As Carrie Frances talks, she hears in her mind a gunshot and footsteps running on dry, cut field grass. She smiles and says, "I told you about us going out together when he forgave me." Viola replies, "Yeah, and you said he couldn't do it like he used to." She explains, "It wasn't that he couldn't get it up and bang. He just didn't want to learn anything new. Viola, I did everything in the book about sex to that man. He enjoyed it so much that he howled like a coyote." Laughing she continues, "But he didn't want to return the favor. He said, 'I can't get used to this.' I told him that I couldn't be his wife if he couldn't do that. I really would have married him then, if the sex was good. When he takes me to the movie, I am going to ask him if he thinks he can get used to my way now." Carrie Frances bursts out laughing. Viola, laughing so hard, says, "Oh, I almost forgot, Caesar is home. He looks good, just like the same little Caesar." Carrie Frances in a sweet, sincere voice says, "I would love to see Caesar. I haven't seen Caesar since we were in grade school. Do you remember when he came to school with that patched up haircut his great-grandma Mrs. Seeley gave him?" Viola says, "No, tell me about it."

Caesar's Haircut

Caesar is brown-skinned, with slightly curly hair. He is eight years old and extremely small in height and size. Caesar is wearing old man dungarees. He has patches of hair cut out all over his head. Ms. Dylon, with a devilish smile, sees Caesar's haircut and says, "Caesar! Come here." Caesar, ashamed and scared, walks up to the teacher's desk. Stuttering he asks, "Y-yes m-ma'am?" Ms. Dylon asks, "Who cut your hair?" Stuttering, he says, "Mm...my gr...great-grandma." Laughing, Ms. Dylon says, "Caesar, wait here."

Caesar waits by Ms. Dylon's desk, looking scared. Ms. Dylon goes out of the classroom and returns immediately with Ms. Bammer, the fourth-grade teacher, and they stand by the desk. Ms. Dylon, laughing and pointing at Caesar's hair, says, "Look, Bammer, he said his great-grandma cut it. A new style." Ms. Bammer looks at Caesar's haircut and begins to laugh, "Uh, uh, ha," holding her stomach and laughing uncontrollably. Ms. Bammer laughs so hard that she has to be carried out of the room into the hallway and slapped to stop her from laughing. (End of Flashback)

Carrie Frances says, "She said her tickle box turned over and wouldn't stop. That's why they had to slap her." Viola, laughing hysterically, says, "Well, my tickle box is turning over now." Carrie Frances, laughing, says, "Well, you haven't heard it all yet. Did you know that Mrs. Seeley used to hitch Caesar out?" Viola says, "What! You mean really hitched him?" Carrie Frances says, "Yeah, I remember the first time I saw Caesar hitched out. I was about five years old."

Caesar is Hitched Out

Carrie Frances is in the backseat of the car. Her father, Wallace, a handsome forty-three-year old, fair skinned man and her mother, Flora, are in the front seat. The car is passing Mrs. Seeley's house, an old shack, on Ron Bopkins Highway. Mrs. Seeley is about a hundred years old and in the backyard. She is wearing a long dress dragging on the ground, a pair of old laced-up boots, a bonnet, and a pair of old wire-rimmed glasses. Carrie Frances says, "Momma, look, Caesar is hitched out. Why is he hitched out?" Caesar is in the front yard playing, but he has a rope tied around his waist. The rope is also tied to the front porch, but it is not long enough to reach the road. Mrs. Flora smiles and says, "Well, Mrs. Seeley don't want him to run out into the road. When Caesar was really little, he ran out into the road and a car hit him and knocked him clean up in the air. She don't want him to get hurt again." (End of Flashback)

Carrie Frances tells Viola, "Mrs. Seeley hitched Caesar out until they moved over near us. They moved into Miss Tru Cailey's old house. She was the same age as Miss Tru Cailey and Miss Calice Shields." Viola explains, "Carrie Frances, you see, you all had a car, so you saw more stuff than I did. I only saw things that was in walking distance."

Carrie Frances hears a knock at the front door and says, "Viola, someone's knocking on my door. I don't know who it could be. I didn't lock my gate. Hold on."

She goes to the door. It's Benjy, a Caucasian, handsome fortyish, well-built, muscular police officer, and also her boyfriend. She kisses Benjy and gives him a sign that she is on the phone. She goes back into the kitchen and, lying, she says to Viola, "Viola, I have to go. Some friends of mine stopped by from New York for a little while. They are on their way to St. Helena Island, South Carolina, to visit their family for the holidays. I'll talk to you tomorrow."

Benjy takes his hat off and acts just like he's home. They kiss passionately in the kitchen. In one breath he tells her, "I am sorry about your mother, darling;

and what took you so long to come back home?" She tells him, "I had to stay away for a while. I promise I won't stay away that long again." He tells her that he's been looking out for her house and she says, "I know, thanks." All the while giving him that million-dollar smile. He flashes one back on her and asks in that sexy southern voice, "Can I come back when I get off duty?" She replies, "You better." Then he asks her, "What do you want to eat?" All flustered, she answers, "My favorite." With that sexy voice, he says, "Okay, I'll see you in a little bit." He pulls Carrie Frances to him, kisses her, and walks out the door. She closes the door with love on her face.

Bufus Jumps the Fence

Next morning, Benjy and Carrie Frances are having breakfast. They are feeding each other. A knock is heard at the front door. Benjy and Carrie Frances are shocked. They look at each other. She asks, "Didn't you lock the gate last night?" He answers, "Yes, I did. Stay here, let me handle this." He reaches for his gun. Carrie Frances stands back, looking frightened.

He looks out of the front door window and says to her, "I know this guy. Do you know him?" She looks out and says, "Yeah, that's Bufus. He's like my god daddy. How did he get in?" She pauses for a second and says, "He climbed the fence." Benjy shakes his head and says, "Looks like it." She tells Benjy to let him in. He opens the door and says, "Hi, Mr. Bufus." Carrie Frances is thinking something is wrong since he jumped her fence. She says, "Hey, Bufus, it's good to see you. Is everything all right?"

Bufus, a Caucasian man in his seventies, wearing glasses and regular clothes, enters the living room, looking ashamed and nosy, replies, "I tried calling this morning, but I didn't get an answer. So, I drove by and I noticed the car in the yard. I thought something was wrong, so I climbed the fence." Carrie Frances and Benjy look at each other. Bufus looks at Benjy and asks, "What are you doing here, Benjy?" He answers, "Carrie Frances is my girlfriend." Bufus says, "Oh, I forgot you got a divorce a few years back." He pauses for a second and says, "Don't you go with a lady on the police force too?" Carrie Frances interrupts and says, "We were having breakfast; come and join us." He replies, "I don't mind if I do."

The three of them go into the kitchen. Benjy gets a plate and fixes Bufus some food while Carrie Frances pours juice and makes a cup of tea for him. In a way they are like a happy family. Carrie Frances tells Bufus that she is glad he stopped by even though he jumped her fence. Bufus, with a mouth full of food, tells her, "My wife is not home. She's in New Jersey visiting her daughter." He pauses, smells the tea, and asks, "What kind of tea is this? It smells like burnt wood chip." Carrie Frances smiles and says, "It's lapsang souchong." He frowns and asks, "What kind of name is that?" She says, "It's an Oriental tea." He sips his tea and replies, "Taste like burnt wood chip to me." After a few more sips he smiles and says, "Ummm, it's good!" As he continues sipping his tea, with a serious look and tone, he asks her, "Carrie Frances, have you been to see your aunt Colly?" She tells him, "No, not yet but I am going. I have to take her a teakettle. The last time I talked to her, she asked me to bring her a teakettle. I bought it yesterday when Caleb and I went to Walmart. You know, when an old person tells you to buy something for them, you buy it." Benjy joins in and says, "Yeah, I know about that. I bought my granddaddy everything he asked for before he died." He smiles and continues, "The last thing he asked for was some chewing tobacco." He looks at Bufus with a serious look and says, "Mr. Bufus, Carrie Frances and I have been courting for over ten years." Bufus, still eating, slyly and boldly says, "Yeah, I know." He pauses for a second and continues, "You know, Billy Cane is a good friend of mine too and he don't keep no secrets." Carrie Frances and Benjy look at each other but don't say anything. Bufus, still not looking at them, continues, "These grits are good. Got any more?" Benjy gets up and puts more food on Bufus's plate and tells Carrie Frances that he is going to get dressed. She tells him that after she finishes the dishes, she and Caleb are going to clean her parents' grave. Bufus is eating as if he is so hungry. He says to Carrie Frances in a serious tone, "Don't forget to go and see your aunt Colly."

A few hours later Carrie Frances and Cousin Caleb are at the cemetery. Caleb is putting a rake and a hoe into the trunk of the car. He has cleaned her parents' grave. Carrie Frances is now off to see Aunt Colly.

Aunt Colly is very sick, lying in a hospital bed in her bedroom. Carrie Frances feels so bad seeing her aunt so sick. She kisses her and asks, "Aunt Colly, how are you? I bought you a teakettle." Aunt Colly answers in a weak voice, "I do pretty well. You didn't forget, did you?" She answers sadly, "No I didn't." Aunt Colly looks up at her and asks, "How long are you going to be here?" She replies, "Until January 4th, after New Year." Aunt Colly forces a smile and says, "Um, a long time."

Aunt Colly's daughter, Mae Evelyn, comes into the room to give Aunt Colly her medicine. Carrie Frances kisses her aunt and tells her, "Aunt Colly, I'll be back later. I love you." Aunt Colly replies, "I love you too."

3
LIVINGSTON GETS ARRESTED

Carrie Frances enters her house all dressed up. She is just returning from having dinner at Aunt Colly's house. She is very tired and anxious to get out of her clothes and put something on comfortable. The phone rings and it's Viola. She tells her to hold on. Carrie Frances hurries and changes clothes because she is as anxious to gossip as Viola. She comes back and picks up the phone and says, "I am back. I feel comfortable now." The first thing out of Viola's mouth was, "Did you talk to Billy C yet?" She replies, "No, I have to call and wish him a Merry Christmas, and of course, ask him to take me to the movies." A beep is heard on the phone. Carrie Frances tells Viola to hold on so she can answer the other call.

It's her god brother Livingston on the line. Carrie Frances smiles when she hears his voice and says, "Hello, Brotha Livingston." Livingston, very excited, says, "Sistah, sistah, Merry Christmas, my dear. I am in

New York for a while. I'll stop by and bring you your gifts."

For a moment, she can visualize him in her mind's eye.

Livingston, a handsome, well-dressed, flamboyant, tall, fortyish dark-skinned man with very short cropped blond hair and green eyes, is standing in his well-furnished living room talking on the phone. In the background you can see several gifts, beautifully wrapped. Carrie Frances comes back to reality and continues talking to her brotha Livingston saying, "Oh, my brotha, I am in South Carolina for the holidays." He replies, "Good, I can get on a plane and be there in a couple of hours. I really want to see you." She is upset and replies, "Oh no, don't go through all of that trouble. You enjoy your family and I'll see you as soon as I get back." Livingston, disappointed but laughing, says, "Well, all right, I guess you have some man in your den." Carrie Frances is happy now and tells him, "I love you. I'll call you soon. I have my classmate on the line." Livingston with a slight laugh says, "Enjoy yourself."

Carrie Frances flashes back over and laughing says, "Viola, I am so sorry for leaving you on hold for so long but that was my god brother, Livingston." She sighs and says, "Yeah, he wants to come here to visit me. He lives in Los Angeles and New York, but he is back in New York for the holidays." Viola asks, "Why don't you let him come here? It'll be nice to have a new man in town. I would love to meet your god brother. Now, I am not trying to get fresh, but Maggie Mae would." Carrie Frances, smiling, says, "Well, Viola, the town is not ready for him."

Viola asks, "What you mean?" Carrie Frances reluctantly replies, "Well, you see, he's on the other side of the track and besides, he might go to jail for speeding. He drives awful fast." Viola says, "Now, Carrie Frances, you have to do better than this. We have been friends since we were babies. Now give me the whole story." She replies, "Well, you see, we do the same kind of work, and a few years ago we were in Arizona and he got arrested for speeding." Viola, very serious, says, "Carrie Frances, I want the story now. I don't care how long it takes and what do you mean on the other side of the tracks?" She says, "You know I have to call Billy C." Viola anxiously says, "Carrie Frances, I am waiting, I want to hear it all, nonstop in every detail." Carrie Frances, smiling, says, "Well, all right! Here it goes; all of it from start to finish."

Livingston and Carrie Frances, in their late thirties: both are very well dressed. Carrie Frances has her hair in long braids. Livingston's hair is still extremely short and blond. They are walking in a shopping mall in Tucson, Arizona, looking for a pair of Michael Jordan sneakers for Livingston. Carrie Frances is upset with Livingston and says, "Livingston, we've looked all over for those sneakers. I have to go and buy some perfume." Livingston said, "Sistah, let's go in here. If they don't have them, I promise, we'll go and get your perfume." He thinks for a second and says, "You just want to buy some perfume so you can smell sweet for all of those guys on the set that you invite over to your den." Carrie Frances frowns and says, "Livingston, leave me and my men alone." Instantly she smiles and says, "They enjoy coming over to my den." He sucks his teeth and says, "Carrie Frances, get in here." Carrie Frances walks closely behind him. He is practically pulling her.

A very handsome Caucasian man with dark hair, a medium build, in his late thirties walks over to Livingston and Carrie Frances and asks, "Can I help you, sir?" Livingston says, "Yes, I am looking for a pair of Michael Jordan sneakers, size eleven." Before the clerk can answer, Carrie Frances interrupts. Looking at the store clerk, she says, "I hope you have those Michael Jordan sneakers because my brotha Livingston has been dragging me all over this shopping mall. Besides, I have to buy me some perfume." The store clerk smiles. Livingston is upset because he knows Carrie Frances is flirting in her own way. Besides, truth be told, Livingston wants to flirt with the store clerk himself. Livingston, very upset, says, "Sistah, how dare you. This man doesn't need to know about your perfume." The store clerk can barely keep from laughing out loud. Carrie Frances replies, "Well, I didn't mean any harm. I just wanted him to know how bad I wanted you to get your sneakers, and besides, I am quite sure this gentleman can appreciate a woman smelling sweet." She looks at the man, smiles, and says, "Your cologne smells really nice. What's the name of it?" Livingston has had enough and grabs Carrie Frances by the arm and says, "Sistah, I am going to kill you." The store clerk cannot hold it in any longer. Laughing, he says, "It's Ralph Lauren cologne. I am glad you like it." Carrie Frances smiles. The store clerk smiles and says to Livingston, "Sir, we are out of size elevens. I will order the size you want but you will have to pick them up before 7 PM Monday." Livingston says, "Thanks so much. I will see you Monday."

Livingston is so furious with Carrie Frances that he leaves her in the mall. By the time Carrie Frances gets to the parking lot, Livingston is in the car. Carrie Frances is trying to open the car door as he is driving off. He slows down long enough for her to get into the car. He continues driving off before she can close the door, all the while saying, "Sistah, you're a Jezebel tramp. What do you be doing to those men? If you had stayed back there a little while longer, that man would have been coming to your den also." She smiles and says, "What do you expect? Your sister is gorgeous." He replies, "Ahh!" Livingston and Carrie Frances speeds toward Benson, Arizona.

The following Monday at Mescal Fort in Benson, Livingston and Carrie Frances are tidying up their stations in the hair-and-makeup trailer. He says to her, "Sistah, hurry up. I have to go to Tucson to get my sneakers." She tells him, "I don't want to go. Take me to the hotel first." He says, "I don't believe you don't want to flirt with your new den partner, or do you have another date with someone from the set?" Lying, she says, "No, I just want to go to the hotel. I am tired." Moments later Livingston is driving out of the parking lot with Carrie Frances trying to close the door. Upset, Carrie Frances says, "Livingston, why can't you ever wait until I get into the car completely before you take off." He replies, "When I am driving, you should be in the car waiting for me." Carrie Frances, with a sad look on her face, says, "Livingston, please take me to the hotel. It's only three minutes away." He replies, "No!"

Livingston turns right onto Highway 43, headed to Tucson, speeding. He is driving 110 miles per hour. Carrie Frances is so scared that she is praying to herself and watching the speedometer. She softly says, "Livingston, you're doing 110 miles per hour and you just passed the po-lice." Livingston sarcastically says, "So!" Livingston is speeding steadily toward Tucson. She is still praying. Livingston constantly looks through his rearview mirror and says softly, "Sistah, what's that light doing flashing at us." Carrie Frances looks back and says, "Livingston! That's the po-lice." With a firm voice, she tells him, "Livingston, when that po-lice stops you, be on your best behavior. Do whatever he says. Speak calmly and answer yes and no to him. And please, do not ask him why he stopped you." He interrupts with the word "Why?" She looks at him with a serious look and says in a firm voice, "Livingston! Haven't you ever heard of po-lice brutality? Livingston, we are in Benson, Arizona. In the middle of the desert and we are black. There is only one black person here in Benson. He is married to a white woman and he is also half Apache. That po-lice could kill us and throw us over there in those bushes. No one will ever find us. Use your head." Livingston pulls over.

The police officer gets out and walks up to the driver's side of the car. The first words out of Livingston's mouth are "What did I do, Officer? I didn't do nothing."

Carrie Frances can't believe what he is saying. She is frightened out of her wits. The police officer tells him, "Sir, step out of the car." Livingston says, "Officer, I didn't do nothing." Carrie Frances in a firm, low voice says, "Livingston, get out of the car, put your hands up, and do what the officer tells you."

Livingston gets out of the car and leans onto the car with his hands up. The officer has his gun drawn. He takes Livingston's wallet out of his pocket. He handcuffs him and escorts him to the patrol car. Livingston gets into the backseat of the patrol car. The officer walks back to the rear of Livingston's car and says, "Miss, please step out of the car." Carrie Frances crying and in a soft voice says, "No! You might shoot me. When I reach for the door, you'll think I am reaching for a gun. Then you'll shoot me and my brotha and throw us over there in the desert. Nobody will ever find us. Then I won't be able to see my kids nor my momma again." The police officer shakes his head and says in a soft voice, "Miss, I promise you, I won't shoot you." Carrie Frances, still crying, in a soft voice asks, "You promise?" The officer replies softly, "Yes, I promise."

Carrie Frances, still frightened and crying, says, "Okay, I am putting my right hand on the door handle. I am opening the door. I am getting out of the car. I've got both hands up. Please don't shoot me." The officer says with a smile, "You see, I told you I wouldn't shoot you. Do you have a driver's license?" She answers softly and sad, "Yes, it's in the car." The officer tells her, "Go and get your license." She goes to the car, gets her purse, comes back, and hands it to the officer. The officer tells her nicely, "You can go in your purse and get your license." She takes her license out of her purse and hands it to the officer. She glances at Livingston sitting in the back of the patrol car, looking sad; she feels so bad for her brotha that it almost brings her to tears. The officer says, "You have a New York driver's license too." Carrie Frances, all bad now, says, "Well, what do you expect? We live in New York." He asks, "Well, what are you doing out here in Arizona with a rental car rented by a production company? What is that, a production company?" Carrie Frances is really bad now. Hands on her hips, she says, "We make movies. We come from all over the world. Just because we work in different states; we can't get a new driver's license in every place we work." The officer says, "Well, I have to run a check on your license."

The officer goes back to his patrol car and runs a license check. He walks back over to her and says, "You're squeaky clean too." She replies, "Well, what do you expect?" The officer explains, "I thought you all were gun runners and drug smugglers because you were driving so fast." Carrie Frances is really upset now and says, "Gun Runners and Drug Smugglers! We are working folks. We don't Run no Guns and Smuggle no Drugs." Crying she says, "Besides, my brotha was driving fast so he could get to Tucson before 7 PM, so he could get his Michael Jordan sneakers." The officer says, "Well, I am sorry about that. I have to take him in." Hysterically she says, "You can't do that. I need my brotha to help me do those wigs. I have twenty-three wigs to do tomorrow. I can't do all of that work by myself." Extremely hysterically she continues, "You can't lock my brotha up. I can't do the movie by myself." The officer feels sorry for her and says, "Well, he'll have to pay a fine." Carrie Frances reaches into her ladies bank and pulls out a $10,000.00 roll and very excited says, "Okay, here, how much? I'll pay." The officer is shocked and says, "I can't take this money out here. You'll have to pay at the precinct. Your brother rides with me. You can follow in his car." Smiling she says, "Oh, all right." The police officer takes off, speeding at eighty miles per hour.

Carrie Frances is afraid to drive too fast. She doesn't want to get arrested for speeding and says to herself, "That po-lice is crazy. He's driving eighty miles per hour. I am not driving that fast and let him arrest me for speeding." Carrie Frances follows the car to the turnoff to Benson. She realizes the car she is following is a taxi the same color as the patrol car, and thinks, Oh, my god! That's not the police officer's car, that's a taxi. She is totally lost and pulls up beside the taxi and asks for directions. She tries to follow the directions that were given to her.

As she passes a motel, she realizes she is totally lost. She turns around and drives into the motel parking lot near the manager's office.

Carrie Frances walks up to the manager's door. The motel manager is an old Caucasian lady who comes to the door with a shotgun. Carrie Frances, in a frightened voice, says, "Ms. I need your help. I am lost. The police stopped me and my brother out on Highway 43, going to Tucson, for speeding." Practically out of breath she continues, "The po-lice arrested my brother and told me to follow him. The po-lice was driving too fast for me to keep up, so I am lost. I don't know where the precinct is."

The old lady puts down her shotgun, smiles, and in a heavy voice says, "Honey, don't you worry. Go out there and make a left turn. Go down two blocks, make another left and go about four blocks. Don't be afraid, you are going to go up and downhill, and it's very dark." She takes a breath and continues, "Don't worry. Then you will come to a street that's well-lit on your right. Make a right turn and the precinct is on your left. Don't go to the front door because at night they don't use that door. Go around to the back and ring the bell. Don't be scared, go on." Carrie Frances smiles and says, "Thank you so much." She follows the directions and goes directly to the precinct.

As Carrie Frances rings the bell, she hears Livingston saying, "I told you my sistah was coming." She is buzzed in and as she walks down the hall she starts talking to Livingston before she sees him. She says, "Brotha Livingston, I would have been here a long time ago, but the officer drove so fast I couldn't keep up with him, so I got lost." Livingston is big and bad now that his sistah is there, so he says, "You see, you should lock yourself up. You were speeding and lost my sistah." The police officer ignores what Livingston said and gives Carrie Frances a receipt that he had already written out. Carrie Frances and Livingston leaves.

Carrie Frances drives this time. The drive isn't far, but Livingston is very quiet and appreciative. She takes him to his hotel room first, which is just across the courtyard from her room. Immediately, she walks across the courtyard and is so happy to get back to her den as Livingston calls it.

The next day at work, Livingston and Carrie Frances are riding in a van down the road with several actors and crew members. Livingston sees the policeman who is guarding the set as the van drives by; The policeman is leaning up against his patrol car. Loudly, Livingston yells, "Sistah, there's that policeman who arrested us last night." Carrie Frances laughs and says, "Arrested us? You mean, arrested you." He says, "I am going to give that officer a piece of my mind."

The van arrives at the set. Livingston and Carrie Frances run back to the officer. Carrie Frances all big and bad says, "Yeah, you're that officer that arrested my brotha last night." Out of breath from running she says, "I told you we weren't no Gun Runners and Drug Smugglers." The surprised police officer looks at Carrie Frances and says, "I was afraid that you all were. I thought I might never see my wife and kids again." Carrie Frances, with a non-believing look, says, "Well, in that case, why did you stop us by yourself? You should have called for backup." The officer then said in a sweet voice, "Well, I was afraid for you. Had I not stopped your brother he might have killed you driving that fast." She smiles sweetly and says, "Well, if you say so." Livingston hears that and becomes upset and says, "I don't believe it, you're flirting with him. I guess he'll be in your den tonight."

As Livingston and Carrie Frances walk back down

the road toward the set, Carrie Frances looks back at the police officer and they smile at each other. Livingston sees this and playfully smacks Carrie Frances; They walk back to the set and start doing touch-ups on the actors' hair. (End of Flashback)

Carrie Frances realizes that Viola is not on the phone, so she says, "Viola, Viola, are you there?" Meanwhile, at Viola's house. Viola is a brown-skinned, semi-heavyset woman in her forties with short hair pinned back with bobby pins. Viola is literally lying on the floor laughing, crying, and kicking from shock of the story that Carrie Frances is telling. Viola's husband, Vernest, and their teenage kids are standing in the doorway looking at her. She sees her husband and kids and feels ashamed. She gets up and wipes tears of laughter from her eyes.

Back at Carrie Frances's house she can hear Viola's husband in the background on the phone saying, "Every time Carrie Frances comes home, you two are on the phone all day and night laughing from her telling you stories, but I have never seen you act like this. This one takes the icing off the cake."

Viola's husband and kids goes back into the living room laughing and shaking their heads in disbelief. Viola, wiping her eyes and laughing, comes back to the phone and says, "Carrie Frances, was he really going to get some Michael Jordan sneakers and got arrested?" She replies, "Yes, he was." Viola says, "Carrie Frances, you must have plenty of stories to tell about the things you've done and the people you met since you left here. That's why I love calling you when you come home. Even if I don't see you, at least I can talk to you. You make me laugh. This town is boring." She replies, laughing, "I know it is. Maybe I'll have a story-telling party and invite Maggie Mae and Caleb. I can't invite anyone else, because I don't want everyone knowing my business." Viola says, "Carrie Frances, all of us would love that. Carrie Frances, did you take that police officer to your den after work?" She smiles and says, "Yes, I did, and I enjoyed myself." She pauses and says, "A thousand times better than Billy C." Laughing, she says, "On that note, I have to call my honey now. Viola, I'll talk to you later."

Billy C

Carrie Frances calls Billy C. He answers in a soft tone. "Hello." She says, "Billy C, hey, how are you? It's me, Carrie Frances." She senses something is wrong and she asks, "Am I interrupting you or did I call at a bad time?" He answers, "No." Carrie Frances says, "Merry Christmas to you." He replies, "Merry Christmas to you, too. Did the kids come with you?" She says, "No, Billy C. I sneaked off from them. I felt I needed to make this trip by myself. How are your kids?" He replies, "They are fine." She asks, "Do they live here in town?" He says, "No, they live in Lawrence." She then says sadly, "You know, Billy C, I was very sick after Momma died. In July, I had surgery on my knee." Laughing she continues, "I was walking around on crutches for about four months. It took me about an hour to walk somewhere, when, normally it took only ten minutes, but I am okay now." He goes on to say,

"I've been sick myself with a cold. I am taking antibiotics." The doorbell rings at Billy C's house and he tells her, "Hold on, I have to answer the door." She replies, "Okay, I'll hold."

When he comes back to the phone he says, "I have to hang up. I have to make a phone call." Carrie Frances is upset and says, "I can understand you have company. Do you have my phone number?" He answers, "No." She asks, "Well, do you have time to write it down before you make your phone call?" Billy C replies, "No." She then asks, "Well, do you want to get it from Ola Jean or Loletha, or do you want me to call you back and give it to you?" He says, "No." Teary-eyed, Carrie Frances says, "Well, I'll talk to you later." She hangs up the phone in a daze. She is so out of it that she doesn't think about locking the outside gate.

Carrie Frances is heartbroken and lies down on the sofa with her clothes on. She falls into a deep sleep. She attempts to get up twice to go to bed realizing it's late. She is going into a spirit realm; her spirit is trying to tell her something. Sometimes it tells her things when she is wide awake and at other times in her sleep. This is one of those times that she needs to be asleep. She is in such a deep sleep that she cannot get up. On the third attempt, she looks at the clock and it's 5:30 a.m. She forces herself to go into her bedroom, take off her clothes, and put on a gown. She gets into the bed and it's now 5:45. Carrie Frances dreams.

Dream Sequence

Carrie Frances enters a hotel room and begins

hanging up her clothes in the closet. She looks back and sees an adjoining room with a dead person in bed with their knees up underneath the covers. She realizes that the killer is hiding behind the door in the adjoining room. In her mind's eye, Carrie Frances can see the person who is hiding. She runs out of the room into the hallway of the hotel and thinks, I don't want nobody to think I killed that person. Oh, my god, my clothes are in there. I have to get my clothes.

Carrie Frances sees a hotel maid, a young Caucasian girl with long, wavy dark hair, pushing a cart. Carrie Frances says to her, "Can you stay out here in front of this room until I get my things and come back out?" Excited, the young maid says, "Sure." Carrie Frances goes back into the room to get her clothes. Immediately upon entering the room, she sees with her mind's eye from the hotel room window a Caucasian male, hotel manager standing at the bottom of the outdoor stairs that leads to the second floor of the hotel. The manager looks up at Carrie Frances and yells to the young maid, "Who's that in the room?" The young maid replies, "That lady asked me to wait here until she gets her things out of the room." Carrie Frances sees and hears this with her mind's eye, and she thinks, I am not waiting around. They can keep these clothes and shoes. I am not going to get blamed for killing someone that I didn't kill. Carrie Frances runs out of the room. (End of Dream)

Carrie Frances awakes from her dream. She hears a knock at her front door. She's startled because her front gate is supposed to be locked.

Carrie Frances realizes that she had forgotten to lock the gate the night before because she was so upset by Billy C's conversation with her. She looks out of the door window and sees that it's one of her high school sweethearts, Thames. She says to him, "You were supposed to call me first." He replies a little embarrassed, "I was passing by and I saw the gate open, so I came on in and knocked."

Carrie Frances and Thames go into the kitchen and sit at the table. She makes coffee and gives him some corn pudding that she had made the day before. They haven't seen each other in years. Thames looks at her and says, "You are so pretty." She replies with a smile, "Really, thank you." He goes on to say, "I always thought you were the prettiest girl that I had ever met." He notices some pictures that are on the kitchen table and asks, "Can I look at these pictures?" She replies, "Yes, they were taken on my last job." He looks through the pictures. He takes one of the pictures of her, kisses it, and places it next to his heart. Carrie Frances is blown away by this and begins to think of Billy C. Why can't Billy C and I be like this? We used to. The nerve of him to let someone come between our friendship. I am going to call him and tell him so. Carrie Frances comes back to reality and asks Thames, "How long do you have off for the holidays?" Thames, still holding the photo, says, "I go back early in the morning. I know you are still sleepy." She answers, "Yes, I didn't get to bed until 6 a.m." He says, "I just stopped by. I wanted to see you so bad. I promise the next time I'll call." She tells him, "You can't have this picture, but

I will give you one at another time." She walks him to the door and comes back to tidy up the room.

Immediately, she hears another knock at the front door. This time it is Devin Gadson and his brother on their way to St. Helena Island, South Carolina.

Carrie Frances says, "You finally showed up. Come on in." Devin kisses Carrie Frances and says, "Left late, Joe wanted to party last night." Joe says, "Hi, Carrie Frances, I am sorry about that." "She replies, "It's all right, at least you stopped by. Come on in, let me feed you guys." Devin and Joe sit in the living room while Carrie Frances brings out food and drinks. They sit around laughing and talking for a long time and then it is time for them to leave. As Devin and Joe are leaving, Devin comes back and gives Carrie Frances a big kiss, smack in the mouth. She is happy he kissed her. They smile at each other and Devin is off to see his family.

4

REVELATION OF DREAM/ BILLY C IS DEAD

Late evening, Carrie Frances is lying on the sofa in her living room. The telephone rings and she answer's; it's Viola. She is still in a mood about Billy C, so she is a little down when she says, "Hello, Viola!" Viola, in a concerned voice, says, "Carrie Frances, I don't want to upset you but how did Billy C sound when you talked to him last night?" She is a little sad and replies, "Well, I started to call you back last night and also call Ola Jean and Loletha too. Billy C refused to take my telephone number. I know he had company. I could tell somebody was there when I first called him. Then, his doorbell rang."

Viola cuts Carrie Frances off and says, "They say he killed himself last night. Ola Jean just found his body about fifteen minutes ago." Carrie Frances' eyes widen with shock and she says in a serious tone, "No, Viola, he wouldn't do that." She thinks about the dream and says, "Oh my god! That's what my dream was about."

Carrie Frances is losing it. All kind of thoughts are going around in her mind. She can't believe it. She came home especially for Billy C. She wanted to rekindle their relationship. She wanted to show him her name on the screen credits. She wanted to stay with him if he could bang it all right. She cries uncontrollably. Carrie Frances, crying, says, "Viola, somebody was in the house with him while I was talking to him on the phone." Viola, real concerned, asks, "Are you going to be all right?" Carrie Frances, still crying, says, "No, no I am not! I can't take this. It's too much. Momma just died the last time I was home." She takes a deep breath and says, "I come home and the man I almost married is dead. Viola, do you remember?"

Carrie Frances Runs Off/ I Don't Want To Get Married

Viola and Jammy are in the backseat of the car making out. Billy C and Carrie Frances are in the front seat arguing. Carrie Frances is saying, "I want to go to New York. I promise I'll come back in two weeks, and we'll get married." Billy C says, "No you won't. You'll get a taste of those bright lights and you'll never come back." She replies, "Take me home now, Billy C." Billy C says, "Not unless you marry me." Viola tells her, "Carrie Frances, marry him." Jammy yells, "Yeah, get out of the car and go and get married."

Minutes later on Billy C's front porch. Ola Jean says, "You all are just having a lovers' quarrel." Mrs. Sue Hattie, Billy C's mother, says, "Yeah, get married, and have me a pretty grand baby." Mr. Lit, Billy C's daddy, says, "Yeah, you'll be a pretty daughter-in-law. Go on down to Millon and get married."

Later that night, Billy C and Carrie Frances are driving past the turnoff to Carrie Frances' house. She doesn't want to get married. She has plans to leave for New York with two of her friends at 5:30 tomorrow morning. She tells him softy, "You passed the road to my house." Softly he says, "I know, I am taking you to Millon so we can get married tonight. I am going to prove to you that I love you and the baby you are carrying." She says, "All right, but since I am pregnant, my bladder is weak. I have to pee." Billy C pulls over on the side of the road. He gets out of the car, comes around and opens the door for Carrie Frances. He turns his back to give her privacy. Carrie Frances pretends to pee. She backs up and tiptoes down the road and starts running. Billy C jumps into the car and starts to chase behind her. Carrie Frances is running like a bat out of h-e-ll. Carrie Frances runs toward her house across the field. Billy C continues chasing her with the car.

Mrs. Flora and Mr. Wallace are in bed sleeping. Mrs. Flora hears Carrie Frances' footsteps running across the cut field grass. She jumps up and grabs the shotgun. Mr. Wallace, still lying in bed, says, "Flo, put that shotgun down." Mrs. Flora goes onto the front porch and fires the shotgun up into the air and yells, "Carrie Frances, what's the matter?" Carrie Frances, still running toward her house with Billy C still in pursuit, yells, "I'll tell you when I get there." Mrs. Flora fires again. Billy C stops and backs the car up this time and drives away. Carrie Frances runs up onto the porch, and her mother, upset, out of breath, and at the same time so happy that she is not hurt, asks, "Carrie Frances, what's wrong?" She replies softly, "Nothing." Her father, Mr. Wallace, says, "I told you, there ain't nothing wrong with that youngling." Carrie Frances goes into her bedroom and jumps into the bed with her clothes on. She is not going to let nothing, or no one stop her from leaving. She thinks, 'I hope Billy C don't come back and tell Daddy he wants to marry me. 'Cause, Daddy will tell him, 'Take her, you want me to sign for her?' I can't wait until 5:30 to come. I'll be on my way to New York City'. (End of Flashback)

Carrie Frances is still talking to Viola. In a regretful voice she says, "Viola, had I not run off, we would have been married and he wouldn't be dead." Suddenly she becomes frantic and says, "Viola, my head is hurting. I can't stay by myself. Whoever was in the house with him can get my number from the caller ID and find out where I live. They'll come and kill me."

Viola frantically says, "Carrie Frances, I am scared to drive by his house. Call your cousin Maggie Mae; maybe she can come. In the meantime, I am going to find out what I can about what really happened." Carrie Frances, disappointed, says, "Yeah, I'll call Maggie Mae. She's like a telephone. She knows everything."

Carrie Frances hangs up from Viola and calls Maggie Mae. Maggie Mae's son Gerrod answers the phone. When she asks him if his mother is home, he answers all excited, "No, she's over at Billy C's house trying to find out what happened. I'll tell her you called, and she'll call you back." She replies, "All right,

Gerrod." Carrie Frances puts the phone down and is walking back and forth holding her head.

The phone rings a few minutes later. It's Maggie Mae calling to tell the gossip. She doesn't know about Carrie Frances and Billy C's relationship. When Carrie Frances answers the phone and talking fast says, "Hello, Maggie Mae, I can't stay by myself. Can you come over?" It goes over Maggie Mae's head. She's so into gossip that she really doesn't hear what Carrie Frances says to her.

In order for you to understand what is going on in this town tonight, I have to take you over to Maggie Mae's house. She is in her kitchen gossiping.

Maggie Mae is fortyish, with brown skin, a bumpy face, big lips, stuck-out teeth, and an extremely large bust, hips, and butt. She's five feet, four inches and a loudmouth. She is so into the gossip about Billy C that she doesn't comprehend what Carrie Frances is really telling her. Maggie Mae's son, Gerrod, is fifteen years old, a semi-chubby country bumpkin sitting in the kitchen, all excited about the goings on, watching and listening to his mother tell the gossip about Billy C.

Maggie Mae, with a country voice, excited, says, "Carrie Frances, gurl, der people is out dere tonight all in front of Billy C's house. I don't know what to do." She throws her hand in the air, shakes her head, and says, "Child, we ain't never had nothin' to happen like that here. Child, I am going crazy." She is a little calmer now and says, "I left my sista Poody over dere. She said she's going to keep me posted with her cella phone." Okay, now that you've been introduced to Maggie Mae and her son, I'll take you back to Carrie Frances' house and continue with their conversation. Some of Carrie Frances's past is about to come to light. Here it goes.

Carrie Frances finally gets a word in and says, "Maggie Mae, I have to be honest with you. Billy C and I were closer than most people know. We almost got married when I was in school."

Maggie Mae can't believe what she is hearing and interrupts Carrie Frances. "No! Gurl, hush your mouth."

Carrie Frances continues. "And another thing, I talked to him last night. I am afraid that whoever was in the house last night with him might find out my phone number and where I live from the caller ID. I am scared. Can you come and spend the night with me?"

Maggie Mae says, "I can't come 'cause I have to wash out my uniforms for work. I'll call my brother Caleb to see if he can stay with you."

Carrie Frances replies very gratefully, "That will be good."

She hangs up the phone and waits for Cousin Caleb to call her. She is still upset. Finally, Cousin Caleb calls and says in a serious tone, "Cusin Ker Francie, I hear you need ma hep. I'll be there." Happily, she answers, "Thanks, Caleb."

She hangs up the phone, and Maggie Mae calls back immediately. She tells Maggie Mae, "I spoke to Caleb and he said he will spend the night with me." Maggie Mae replies, "Carrie Frances, I will have Caleb dere in twenty minutes." Carrie Frances is much better now that she'll have someone to stay with her for the night. The reason Carrie Frances is so afraid is that she doesn't have any firepower in her house. I'll let you in on a little secret. In a day or so, even though Carrie Frances is unaware of it, she will have more than enough firepower to sustain almost anything.

Carrie Frances sits down in the living room, looking so sad, and thinks, Viola is scared to drive by Billy C's house. She doesn't know what scared is.

Carrie Frances has flashbacks of ghost stories from her childhood.

Ghost Stories (Hant-Hank)

Carrie Frances is sitting in a chair. Her father, Mr. Wallace, is telling ghost (Hant-Hank) stories from his courting days, when he was a teenager. Mrs. Flora, her mother, looks on and listens. Mr. Wallace tells his story seriously with a smile. "I was a teenage boy going courting, and back in those days, you had to walk about seven to ten miles to go courting at night and walk back home too. One night I was walking by myself, coming around some woods and all of a sudden, I heard something fall from the trees up ahead of me. I was so scared, my hair stood up on my head, but I kept walking. All of a sudden, this man was walking beside me. I kept walking; then I looked down and realized his feet wasn't touching the ground. He was floating." When her father finished, little Carrie Frances, smiling, says, "Daddy, tell me some more hank stories."

Mrs. Flora walks over to the edge of the porch and spits and sits back down. Mrs. Flora takes another dip of snuff, smiles, and says, "Yeah, there were plenty of hanks back then. You don't see them a lot now, because of the electricity." She looks at Wallace and says, "Go on, tell her." Wallace, with a great big grin and a serious tone, says, "The next time I went courting. I went with a group of boys to see these girls. This man and his wife had several girls of courting age. So, we boys went to see them. We were all sitting in the company room when all of a sudden, we heard someone whipping their dogs and you could hear the woman hant saying, 'You owe me money. You didn't pay me for my pigs.' The hant continue to whip the dogs. The dogs were barking and howling from the beating. The girls said that woman hant came every night and beat their dogs, because their father never paid the woman for her pigs before she died." Laughing, Wallace said, "We boys were so scared that we all laid across one bed and stayed until daybreak. Everybody in the house were scared." He looks at little Carrie Frances and says, "A friend of ours lived in a hanted house and every night the hants would come and pump water from their pump." He looks at Flo and says, "Like your momma said, back in those days, there were no electricity and hants were everywhere." Mrs. Flora, with a serious look and tone, says, "When we moved here, this was the most hanked house you ever did see, but Wallace put up horseshoes over the doors and we didn't see or hear anymore hanks." (End of Flashback)

Carrie Frances, still sitting on the sofa, thinks, Billy C hasn't been dead long enough to be a ghost. Viola shouldn't be scared. Momentarily, Maggie Mae pulls up with Caleb and Gerrod. Carrie Frances hurries to the front door. Cousin Caleb gets out of the car with a shotgun wrapped in a blanket and says, "Cusin Ker Francie, I am here to 'tect you. I got ma shotgun, ma bullits in ma pocket. I got ma switchblade and ma straight razor. Ain't nobody gon bother you now." Happily, Carrie Frances replies, "Come on in, cousin. I am so glad you came."

Carrie Frances is feeling better now that she is safe with Cousin Caleb being her bodyguard. She serves Caleb food and soda. They talk for a while and go to bed.

Carrie Frances can't sleep well because she is looking out of the window most of the night. She lives on the main highway; therefore, she can see all of the police cars with sirens blasting as they pass her house. She even sees the coroner passing with her beloved Billy C's body. She cries and finally goes to bed.

Hardware Store

The next morning, Carrie Frances walks into the hardware store. An older 60ish Caucasian male customer is at the counter in deep conversation with the owner, a 50ish Caucasian woman. As Carrie Frances passes the counter near the aisle, she overhears their conversation. The woman is saying, "God, that's really bad. I've been knowing him for such a long time. I don't believe he would kill himself." Carrie Frances realizes they are talking about Billy C. She moves closer back down the aisle to hear better. The woman sees what Carrie Frances is doing and motions for the male customer to follow her to the other end of the counter. Carrie Frances pretends to be looking at something.

She can still hear a little and moves to the opposite side of the aisle to hear better, still looking at things to buy.

The woman, in a low voice, says, "Well, tell me this, did they catch anyone?" The male customer realizes Carrie Frances is eavesdropping and speaks in a low voice as well. "Yeah, they said they are holding a woman for his murder. They caught her last night. She's a white woman too." The woman is shocked and continues, "My god! Is she from around here?" The male customer goes on to say, "They say she is from over in North Carolina, right across the line on the other side of McPhall, near McClauringberg."

Carrie Frances hears what she wants and goes to the counter. The male customer goes out of the store. The woman comes to wait on Carrie Frances and in a regular tone asks, "How are you today?" Carrie Frances replies, "I am okay, how are you?" She answers sadly, "I am a little upset about what happened to Billy C. It's a shame." Carrie Frances replies, "Yes, it is. I am very upset also. It's terrible for someone to be killed and then it is classified as a suicide." The woman continues, "Well, he hasn't been the same since he and Carrie Frances broke up and got a divorce." Carrie Frances is upset by this and wants to set the record straight and replies, "No, his ex-wife Carrie Frances didn't have anything to do with him being upset. He forgot about her a long time ago, ever since he caught her in bed with her supervisor at the motel." The woman says, "Your name is Carrie Frances also. Your mother died about a year-and-a-half ago, and you have a house up in Dranchwood, right?" Carrie Frances says, "Yes, and this is my first time coming back since then and to have this happen is almost unbearable." The woman, in a humbler tone, says, "You knew him quite well, didn't you? I remember some years ago, you came in the store and Billy C was in here and the two of you held quite a conversation." Carrie Frances replies in a happier mood, "Yes, I knew him very well and when you saw us talking that time, that was the first time we spoke to each other in about ten years." The woman, apologetic, says, "You know, I thought you were the reason he and his Carrie Frances got a divorce, because he never talked to any woman like he talked to you that day." Carrie Frances is now a little bold and says, "No, I wasn't the reason. Now, Tammy Ann, you know as well as everyone else that Billy C's Carrie Frances was caught in bed with your best friend Grace's husband at that motel. By the way, are they still together?" She replies sadly and ashamed, "No, they divorced shortly after that." The woman is taken aback by Carrie Frances knowing this, smiles, and asks, "Tell me, how did you know that?" Carrie Frances smiles and answers, "Tammy Ann, you should know by now that my cousin Maggie Mae is Miss Darlboro Herald." Carrie Frances and Tammy Ann both laugh simultaneously. Tammy Ann says, "You mean Wilhelmina's daughter?" Carrie Frances replies, "Yes."

Tammy Ann continues, "I didn't know she was a Miss Darlboro Herald but every time I see her, she's always yelling to someone or waving, and she also talks to a lot of men."

Carrie Frances tells her, "That's because she's

looking for a man. She needs a husband."

A customer walks into the hardware store and in a soft, low tone Tammy Ann says, "How many kids does she have? I see her with a carload." Carrie Frances says, "She has five." Tammy Ann says, "Carrie Frances, you take care of yourself. I am so happy we had our little conversation." Carrie Frances answers softly, "I am too. You take care and have a Happy New Year." Carrie Frances leaves the counter and walks toward the door. The male customer walks to the counter and in a regular voice Tammy Ann says, "Sir, will there be anything else?" The customer replies, "No, this is it."

Coming Clean with Benjy

Carrie Frances is lying on the sofa. Benjy enters with an envelope in his hand and takes off his coat. He puts the envelope on the coffee table and comes over and kisses Carrie Frances. With a serious look he says, "I need to talk to you about something." Carrie Frances sits up and says, "Okay." Benjy sits down and says, "I need you to tell me about Billy C." Carrie Frances, with a serious look and tone, says, "We dated prior to my leaving here many years ago. We almost got married. I ran off and left him. Years later we became friends again. He forgave me for running away. Since then, we were like a divorced couple that was on good terms with each other." He tells her, "I can understand that. I feel that way about my ex-wife." She went on to say, "I called him Christmas night to wish him a Merry Christmas, but he didn't talk right. I believe he had company. He didn't talk to me the way he used to.

We always talked nice to each other, regardless of who we were with, because we were friends. I can't believe he is dead. I was afraid to stay by myself last night because I didn't know who was in his house, and being that I called him, my number was on his caller ID. My cousin Caleb came over and spent the night with me." Benjy asks, "Why didn't you call me? I would have checked on you, had I known you were afraid." She told him, "I knew you were busy." Benjy, holding Carrie Frances' hands, tells her, "I'll come by later and bring you something for your protection." He looks at her with a serious look and says, "Now seriously, no one commits suicide and lays the gun on the nightstand. Carrie Frances, he was shot on the right side of his head and the gun was on the nightstand on his left side. A young lady was questioned last night. She lives close, just over the North Carolina border. She works at a motel over there. Billy C and a supervisor from his job met her at a club near the motel. She's also good friends with the motel manager." Benjy is very upset and takes a deep breath and continues, "I know she did it, but I can't go against my superiors. I also found papers that shows he took out a lot of money from his 401(k) and from his bank account. No money was found in his house." Carrie Frances, with a serious look and tone, asks, "How does she look? I need to know in case I run into her." He replies seriously, "I know you need to know, because they are not going to charge her."

Benjy picks up the envelope off the coffee table and hands it to Carrie Frances. She looks through all of the papers and pictures. Benjy tells her, "Everything is in there, her photos, address, home and cell numbers, where she works and hangs out. Also, a photo of her car and license plates is in there too." He takes another deep breath and says, "It's no telling what she made him tell her about you before she killed him. I erased your number from the caller ID." Carrie Frances, absorbing all of the information and looking at photos, says, "Thanks." Benjy gets up to leave and puts on his coat. She hugs him and he tells her, "I'll stop by later and drop off a package for you." Carrie Frances with a sad, happy face smiles. Benjy walks out of the house. She sits back down onto the sofa, leans back, and closes her eyes.

Paying Respect/Gathering Info

Carrie Frances drives into the yard. She sees several cars and lots of people standing outside, including Billy C's ex-wife, Carrie Frances. Carrie Frances parks her car and goes into the house. The living room is packed with people including Billy C's brother and sister-in-law. Carrie Frances is led into the rear room where Ola Jean is sitting. Ola Jean gets up and hugs Carrie Frances. Carrie Frances is there to pay her respects, but also to gather information without Ola Jean being aware of it. The two of them have their conversation.

She asks Ola Jean how she's holding up and she shakes her head and says, "Not good. What about you?" Carrie Frances answers, "Well, I am trying to hang in there. Did Loletha tell you that I called him Christmas night and he didn't talk right?" She answers,

"Yes, she told me." Carrie Frances tells her that she knew somebody was in the house with him. Ola Jean says, "We didn't find any of his money that he had taken from his 401k and his bank account." When she tells Ola Jean that she heard he was dating a girl from North Carolina, Ola Jean looks at her and holds her head down and says, "Yeah, he was. She wanted to get married, but he refused to marry her. This talk about marriage only happened in the past two weeks, since he got sick." Carrie Frances asks her if she has a picture of her and if so, she would like to see how she looks. Ola Jean, lying, says, "No, I don't have any pictures of her." Carrie Frances sees a photo of the same girl that Benjy gave her on the dresser. She pretends she doesn't see it and directs her attention to a photo of Billy C's that is lying face down on the dresser. Ola Jean sees her looking at the photo and responds sadly, "Yes, that's my brother's picture." Carrie Frances picks up the picture and says, "My sweet, sweet handsome love of my life," and kisses the picture. Ola Jean asks her if she wants to see where it happened. She nods yes and they walk into Billy C's bedroom.

Carrie Frances says, "It looks the same as it did the last time I was here. He didn't change it at all." Ola Jean goes on to say, "We had to clean up all of the mess, but besides that it was clean like he always kept it." Carrie Frances responds, "I know, he kept everything so neat and clean." She pauses a few seconds and asks, "Ola Jean, how much money did he take out altogether." Ola Jean looks sad and says, "Two hundred thousand dollars." Carrie Frances says, "So, the money is nowhere to be found." Ola Jean responds, "That's right. It's nowhere in this house."

Carrie Frances has gotten all of the information she needs and is ready to leave and asks, "When is the funeral?" Ola Jean replies, "New Year's Day." Carrie Frances tells her, "I'll see you then." They hug each other and Carrie Frances walks out the door. As she is walking to her car, she hears the other Carrie Frances talking about her to a lady in the yard. Billy C's ex-wife Carrie Frances looks at Carrie Frances' license plates on her car and notices Georgia plates and says to the lady next to her, "She comes from Georgia." The lady in the yard asks, "Who is she?" Billy C's ex-wife says, "I don't know, but I would love to have those clothes and jewelry." When Carrie Frances hears this, it puts a smile on her face. She and Billy C's ex-wife met many years ago when they were in junior high school at the May Day Parade. At that time neither one of them was dating. A short time after Carrie Frances ran off, Billy C started dating the other Carrie Frances. I guess he said, if he couldn't have the girl, why not get someone with the same name. Carrie Frances says to herself, "He really loved me," and drives off.

5

FIREPOWER

Carrie Frances and Benjy are sitting on the sofa. Benjy has a duffel bag on the coffee table. Carrie Frances has everything she needs now. Benjy is pleased that he can help her. He tells her, "You can register this one for your house." Pointing to the duffel bag he continues, "The others, you can do whatever you want to. They are all new."

She thanks him for helping her. He asks her, "How are you holding up? You feel better?" She looks at him and says, "Yes, a lot better, now that you are here and taking care of me." Benjy and Carrie Frances hug each other as they did before, and they kiss passionately.

Late evening, Carrie Frances is sitting at the kitchen table in a bathrobe. She is talking on her cell. She makes several phone calls and talks for a while, then gets up and goes into her bedroom. When she comes out of the bedroom, she's dressed to the nines. She has a large luggage and a smaller one and she goes out the door.

Palmetto Motel Resort

Carrie Frances is in the parking lot of the Palmetto Motel. As she is exiting her car, she notices a well-dressed, Caucasian, blonde female getting into a Rolls Royce. A motel worker is getting into her car also and says, "Good night, Mrs. Shriver." When the blonde female turns to say good night to the motel worker, her and Carrie Frances' eyes meet and there is a sweet, strange look between the two of them.

Carrie Frances continues to the motel and knocks on the motel door. The door opens and she enters the room, where there is a party going on. Two of the women are around Carrie Frances's age. The other two women are older. All of the women look terrific. Teri, smiling, says, "Misses Big Stuff, what's happening?" Grinning, she answers, "Everything is happening, you know that." Teri and Carrie Frances hug. Verlie comes over and hugs Carrie Frances. Baby Doll comes over and gives her a big hug. Tracy comes over and gives her a big hug too. Carrie Frances is hiding her sadness. She is in a protective mood. There is a time and place for every occasion and this one has no place for sadness. She says, "It's been too long since the Unholy Five have been together."

Carrie Frances sits on the sofa in the living room of the suite. Teri takes Carrie Frances's luggage over into an adjoining room of the suite. Verlie fixes Carrie Frances some food. Tracy sits and shakes her head. Baby Doll smiles. Tracy says, "I am so happy to see you, Carrie Frances." She replies, "I am happy to see you too, all of you. I am also happy that all of you took my advice and moved, so when we need to, we can get together quickly." Baby Doll replies, "That's for sure." Verlie asks, "So, how much time do we have to do this?" Carrie Frances says, "I want it done before New Year's." Teri says, "We can do it." Carrie Frances says, "Teri, there's an envelope in that small suitcase with all of the information."

Teri gets up and brings the envelope back and passes it around to each of the girls. Verlie puts the envelope back.

They all sit around talking and Verlie raises her drink and says, "It looks like old times. Honey, it's boring down here." Teri says, "Yeah, it's time for some action."

Tracy says, "We could all use some of that." Baby Doll replies, "It sure is boring, since I can't boost anymore. I wouldn't dare turn another trick after you saved my life, Carrie Frances."

Carrie Frances suggests, "I tell you what, let's all go dancing. No boosting, no tricking; Just have a good time dancing." Verlie yells, "Yeah." Teri yells, "I am down for it." Baby Doll says, "Me too." Tracy asks, "When?" Carrie Frances says, "Right now."

The Unholy Five/Reunion/Flashbacks

The Unholy Five ladies walk into the club looking like beauty queens. Carrie Frances says to the girls, "Well, we are now queens. Our little girls are princesses." All eyes are on the Unholy Five Queens as they walk in and sit at a table. Carrie Frances tells them, "We shouldn't call ourselves the Five Unholy Queens anymore because some of us have gotten religion again." Verlie replies, "Yeah, I sure did after all I went through in New York and you saved my life twice. I had no choice but to become religious." While talking, Verlie has flashbacks.

Verlie's Flashback-1973

A young teenage Verlie is lying in a bed with the covers pulled up to her neck. An older dark-skinned man in boxer shorts and a wool overcoat is pacing the floor. His eyes are gleaming, and he goes into his closet; believe it or not, but there is a pay phone in the closet. The man makes a phone call and is talking to someone. Meanwhile, the door to the room is open. You can see transvestites walking in the hallway. Carrie Frances is a little scared and she senses something is not right. She says to Ish in a low, soft voice, "Let's go." She then says to Verlie in the same low, soft voice, "Verlie, I am going to walk Ish downstairs." Verlie, lying in bed, begins to cry. Verlie, trying to say something, sounds as if her teeth are loose. She says, "Carrie Frances, please don't leave me."

Carrie Frances winks at Verlie and says, "I'll be back soon."

Carrie Frances turns to the man on the phone and says, "I'll be right back. I am going to walk Ish downstairs."

Carrie Frances leaves with Ish and walks halfway down the stairs. She tells Ish to go on downstairs and hold the door open for her. Ish does what she says, not knowing what she is up to. Carrie Frances walks fast up the few steps to the door. Carrie Frances pushes the door open, winks at Verlie, and says, "You see, I told you I was coming back."

Verlie looks so scared. Carrie Frances then says to the man, "Aren't you going to call a man for me so we can have a party?" The man with gleaming eyes says, "Yeah." He goes back to the pay phone in his closet. Carrie Frances goes over to the bed where Verlie is lying down and asks in a low tone, "Can you walk?" Verlie can barely talk. She tries to move. Carrie Frances sees blood on the pillow beneath Verlie's head. Carrie Frances pulls Betsy out and points it at Donnie Picco, the man on the pay phone in the closet, and shoots him. She then picks Verlie up and puts her across her shoulder and kicks the half-closed door open with her left foot. With her left hand, she points Betsy at the transvestites in the hallway looking. She yells to Ish, "Open the door." Carrie Frances, with Verlie over her shoulder, runs down the stairs. Ish has the door open with a frightened look on his face. Carrie Frances fires two more shots upstairs and says to Verlie, "Hang on, Verlie."

Carrie Frances, with Verlie on her shoulder, and Ish runs down the street to her car. Carrie Frances starts the car and drives Verlie to the hospital. Upon arriving at the hospital, Carrie Frances is informed by the doctors that Verlie has a fractured skull and broken jawbones from being beaten with a hammer by Donnie Picco. Verlie had met Donnie Picco, a singer, a month earlier at Schmalls Paradise Night Club on the Upper Westside of Manhattan, New York City. Verlie was only sixteen years old; she graduated high school two years early because of her astounding academic achievements.

(End of Verlie's Flashbacks)

Verlie continues saying, "The second time you saved my life, you moved me down here. I didn't do nothing but go to church." Carrie Frances smiles and says, "So, now you are a good girl." Verlie smiles and says, "Yeah, but I can still do something to help out a friend." Carrie Frances replies, "Yeah, that's true. Driving is not going to hurt you." Teri cuts in and says, "Yeah, girl, you saved all of our lives. We owe you. We'll do anything for you." Baby Doll looks at Carrie Frances and says, "You saved my life and helped me get my three hundred thousand dollars."

Baby Doll's Flashback-New York-1976

Baby Doll is in a vacant lot hiding money in a jar. A hooker sees what Baby Doll is doing and she goes and tells the pimp. The pimp gets the money and beats Baby Doll up. Baby Doll calls Carrie Frances and tells her what happened. A few hours later, Carrie Frances is in the front seat of a car and Baby Doll is in the back seat pretending to be taking care of a John. Baby Doll is crying, telling Carrie Frances what happened, and says, "Carrie Frances, he beat me up and took my money. That slut told on me." Carrie Frances asks, "Which one?" Baby Doll, wiping her eyes, says, "The hussy in the red coat."

Carrie Frances asks, "Do you know where he keeps his stash?" Baby Doll happily says, "Yeah, in the safe in our house." Carrie Frances asks, "Where is the safe?"

Baby Doll gladly tells her, "In the big closet near the fireplace."

Carrie Frances then asks, "Do you still want to leave from here tonight as planned and go home." She replies, "Yeah, but I will not go home broke with nothing to show for it. I've laid on my back and did everything in the book." She pauses for a second and continues, "If I am going home all bruised and abused, I am going to have some money to show for it. Enough where I will never have to hit a lick in a pie factory." Carrie Frances is quiet for a second and says, "Okay, get out of the car and go back and do your normal thing." She thinks for a second and says, "Oh, do you have all of your personal papers?"

Baby Doll says, "Yeah, I keep them on me all of the time, since I was planning on running away." Carrie Frances tells her, "Give them to me now. When you see my car pull up, come over to it, or if you just see me, come over to me in case I am driving another car. It doesn't matter whether you see me in front of your house or anywhere, just come to me. I'll take care of this, don't worry." Baby Doll looks at Carrie Frances and hands her the papers and says, "I know you will. See you soon." Carrie Frances has a far-off look, smiles, and says, "Yeah."

Later that night in front of Baby Doll's house, detectives kicks open the door with guns drawn; The hookers are scared. Three of the detectives goes directly to the closet by the fireplace; They crack open the safe, empty the contents of money, jewelry, and papers.

The detectives tell the girls they are free to go; Baby Doll is the first to leave, running out of the door. Baby Doll runs out onto the street. She sees Carrie Frances across the street and runs straight to her. They get into the car and drives off. Baby Doll is out of breath and asks, "Did you get the hussy that told on me?" Carrie Frances, still driving, answers calmly, "Yeah, I shot her earlier." Baby Doll gives a big sigh of relief and says, "Good! That heifer." Carrie Frances says, "You said you had three hundred thousand dollars in that jar."

Baby Doll answers like a beaten-down child happy that someone was helping her who she could depend on. She says, "Yeah, every week I went to the bank and exchanged my small bills for hundreds so I could put a lot of money in the jar." Her nose is running from crying. She wipes her nose with her hands and says, "The detectives opened the safe." Carrie Frances tells her, "I know, let's pull over here and get some food."

Carrie Frances pulls over and parks. A car pulls up beside her car. A handsome Irish guy gets out with a large bag and a small suitcase. She rolls her window down and with a smile says, "Hello, you can put it in the backseat." The Irish guy is smiling and asks her, "You want something to eat?" She tells him, "Yeah, get the usual for me. Get her ribs and the works." Carrie Frances turns to Baby Doll and tells her, "We are going to my house in Flatbush. You can count your money and I am driving you home tomorrow."

Two days later, in Bilmington, North Carolina, Carrie Frances and Baby Doll pull up to a real estate office all dressed in business attire. A little while later,

Carrie Frances, Baby Doll, and the Realtor pull up to a beautiful eighteen-room mansion on fifteen acres.

When Baby Doll sees the house, her face lights up and she says, "I like this."

Carrie Frances, with a smooth smile, says, "Me too." She turns to the Realtor and says, "We'll take it." The Realtor flashes a smile because it's a cash sale and says, "Good, it's in move-in condition."

(End of Baby Doll Flashbacks)

Baby Doll continues telling the girls, "I haven't boosted or turned a trick since. After I bought the house, I had plenty money left over. I don't ever have to work." She looks at Carrie Frances and says, "Thanks to you, my friend."

Carrie Frances smiles and looks at her Shirley Temple drink.

Teri takes over the conversation and says, "My story is a little different." Carrie Frances replies, "It sure is." Teri continues saying, "I was sneaking out with this married man who I had dated before he got married." She sips her drink and begins telling her story.

Teri's Flashback-New York-1975

Carrie Frances walks into the bar and sees so many people from her hometown that she feels at home. Bee Noody, a tall, thin African American man about nineteen years old, wearing glasses and very well dressed, sees Carrie Frances. He walks over to her and says, "Carrie Frances, hey girl, how are you? It's good to see you."

Carrie Frances, all excited, says, "Bee, I can't

believe it's you. I am so happy to see you. Everybody is here from home." She takes a deep breath and says, "I am doing good." Bee turns and says, "Terry Van, come over here. Look who's here, Carrie Frances." Terry Van, a handsome, well-dressed young twenty-year-old with brown skin and a medium build, walks over, leaving the people he is talking to at the bar.

Terry Van, all smiles, says, "Carrie Frances, everybody hangs out here from home. The guy who owns this place is from Lennettsville." She replies, "What! You serious?" He continues, "Yeah, you know Toffee Bones. Come on, meet his girlfriend Teri." Toffee Bones and Teri are sitting at the bar hugged up and talking. Terry Van, Carrie Frances, and Bee Noody walk over to the bar. Terry says, "Toffee, Teri, meet Carrie Frances. She's from Silo."

They turn around on the bar stool. Toffee is a stylish, tall, handsome man with fair skin, and Teri, is a tall, stylish young woman with a medium build and beautiful brown skin. Smiling, she says, "Hi, it's nice to meet you." Toffee, all smiles and acting all cool but happy to see Carrie Frances, says, "So, you are from Silo. The little town with the big surprise." Toffee and all of the other homeboys see how good Carrie Frances looks and are very pleased. Toffee on the other hand is acting like a big brother. He sees that Carrie Frances is dressed to kill, looking like she stepped out of a magazine with jewelry out of this world. To himself he's wondering if she is working to really make a decent living or if she is running around like some of the other girls. He's thinking, 'If she doesn't have a job, I'll give her one in one of my companies'. So, he drills her with questions. Carrie Frances knows what and why he's doing this, so she doesn't get angry with him. She answers his questions with a smile. Toffee continues, "How long you been here?" Carrie Frances answers, "Two and a half years." He asks, "You working?" Carrie Frances answers, "Yes." Toffee asks, "Where?" She replies, "Wall Street." Toffee is surprised and says, "What! You mean a Silo girl is on Wall Street." She flashes that million-dollar grin as if to say, "I am not stupid," and at the same time the grin means, "I know you are looking out for me and I thank you." Toffee is very pleased now. After hearing that, everyone is happy that Carrie Frances is working on Wall Street. Toffee looks at her and asks, "Well, how did you find us?" She smiles, laughs, and says, "Now that I think about it, it was destiny." He looks at her real hard and says, "What do you mean?" She replies, "Hm, well, I came here tonight with my girlfriend Verlie and her boyfriend Avery Crown and his brother Dud from Lennettsville." Toffee says, "We all know Avery and his brother Dud." Carrie Frances tells them, "Dud is outside talking to someone; he'll be in soon." Teri, smiling and excited, says, "Tell me about this destiny. I like the sound of that." Bee Noody and Terry Van are looking on. Carrie Frances begins her story.

"Okay, one-night last week my girlfriend Verlie called me. She said she wanted me to go out with her and her new boyfriend along with his brother. So, I asked her, 'What happened to Vin?' She said, 'Avery is Vin's cousin.' So, I said, 'Verlie, how can you go with your boyfriend's cousin?' She said, 'Well, he sold me for fifty cents.' I said, 'What! He sold you for fifty cents?' And Verlie said, 'Yeah, Vin wanted to buy some beer and he needed fifty cents. Nobody would lend him the money because he didn't have a job to pay it back. So, Avery said he'd give him fifty cents if he'd give me to him. Vin said he could have me. Then Avery called me and told me that I was his woman now, because he just bought me from Vin for fifty cents because Vin wanted to buy a bottle of beer.'" Toffee, Teri, Bee Noody, and Terry Van are falling out laughing as Carrie Frances tell her story. She continues, saying, "Verlie said, 'That's all I am worth to him. He could have sold me for at least five dollars, but fifty cents, I can't believe it.'" Laughing, Carrie Frances continues, "So, Avery went over to Verlie's house and then, Verlie called me and told me what Vin had done. Right after that, Avery, his brother Dud, Verlie, and I went out riding. Avery asked me where I was from and I said, 'Silo.' Avery laughed and looked at his brother Dud, and Dud started laughing. So, I asked, 'What's so funny?' They said, 'We are from Lennettsville. We used to go to Silo every week to visit our uncle Reo and his children, Charlie Jay Crown and Dumpsy.' I was so excited to hear that. I couldn't believe it. I was in shock and happy to be with some hometown guys. So, Avery and Dud said, 'If you really want to see people from home, we have to take you to the China Bar on Fulton and Vanderbilt. If you don't believe us, just walk in by yourself and you'll see everyone from home.'" Carrie Frances looks at Toffee and says, "So I did. Don't you think this is destiny?" Teri, laughing, says, "Girl, I love you. We are going to be friends for a long time."

Toffee, Teri, Terry Van, Bee Noody, and Carrie Frances all laugh and hug each other. Nicole Dyntch, a dark-skinned, well-dressed young woman with a Bob hairdo from Silo, recognizes Carrie Frances and walks over and join in the fun too.

Teri and Carrie Frances exchange phone numbers. Verlie, Avery, and Dud walk into the bar and everybody is having fun. Suddenly, Toffee's wife walks in, and Teri stays close to her new friend, Carrie Frances, the rest of the night.

A few months later Teri is in bed sleeping. Her little girl is in bed also. Her telephone rings and she answer's in a sleepy voice. Carrie Frances is talking fast and frantically. "Teri, you have to get out of the house now. You must, you and your child. Someone is going to shoot up your house." Breathing heavily, she continues, "I just dreamed it. I am serious, Teri. Please believe me. Within thirty minutes, they'll be there." Scared, Teri asks, "Who is this?" Crying, Carrie Frances replies, "Teri, it's Carrie Frances. Please listen to me. I've been having these dreams since I was a kid. About things that would happen. They all come true. Remember what I told you about destiny?"

Teri tells her, "I believe you. I'll call you later." Teri hangs up the phone and frantically grabs her baby. Teri puts the baby back down. She puts a coat on, grabs her purse and keys. She puts on her shoes and picks up the baby and runs down the stairs and down the street to her car. She gets into the car and drives off.

As Teri turns the corner, she sees lights from a car

on her block. Seconds later Teri hears gunfire. Teri drives, crying, looks at her baby girl, and says to herself, "It sure was destiny. Had I not met Carrie Frances, where would my child and I be now?"

(End of Teri's Flashback)

Teri continues talking to the Unholy Five, saying, "I stayed with Carrie Frances until Toffee came and gave me money to buy a house down here. I've been here ever since." She takes a deep breath and says, "I haven't worked since I moved here. Toffee gave me two million dollars." She looks away with a far-off look and says, "He could afford it. If he could put a gold toilet seat in his bathroom and buy his wife two mansions, that money was nothing, considering I am the mother of his child." Verlie says, "It's so funny how life is." Teri looks at Carrie Frances and says, "All of us are here because of you, Carrie Frances."

Tracy enters the conversation and says, "You got that right. When I met Carrie Frances, she had a three-month-old baby and was pregnant. You could look at her and tell she was a sweet girl."

Tracy Flashback-1974-Brooklyn N.Y.

Tracy, a 26-year-old, fair-skinned woman with an afro hairdo is walking fast. Her three-year-old son, Blaine, is trying to keep up behind her. Carrie Frances comes out of the gate from her house, carrying a shopping bag filled with clothes in her left hand. She is holding her baby in her right arm. She sees little Blaine trying to catch up to his mother. Carrie Frances smiles at little Blaine and he smiles back at her. Carrie Frances says, "Excuse me, miss, your baby is trying to catch up to you." Tracy yells, "His little ass better walk faster." Carrie Frances puts the shopping bag down. She picks up little Blaine in her left arm and walks fast and catches up to Tracy. Carrie Frances, shocked, says, "Miss, here's your baby." Tracy turns around and says, "What! You didn't have to bring him to me. He has to learn to walk fast." Carrie Frances replies, "But he's little." Tracy says, "So!" Carrie Frances remains calm but is concerned. "Why so mean to him? He's only a baby, and why are you in such a rush?" Tracy, out of breath, answers, "I have to hurry home and get my little girl from the baby-sitter. And I just found out that I am pregnant again from a no-good M---F---."

Carrie Frances's eyes widen. "How far do you live?" She answers, "Lenox and East Fifty-First Street." Carrie Frances says, "That's not far, I tell you what, you walk on and carry my shopping bag as far as the laundromat across Clarkson; Your baby can walk slowly with me. I'll keep him until you go and get your daughter from the baby-sitter."

Tracy looks at Carrie Frances as if she's thinking and says, "You live back there by yourself?" Carrie Frances says, "Yeah." Tracy responds, "Nice house." Carrie Frances says, "Yes, it is." Tracy is calmer now and says, "I guess my baby-sitter can wait a little longer."

Tracy goes back and gets Carrie Frances's shopping bag. Carrie Frances and Tracy walk slowly and talk. As they walk down the street, the usual little neighborhood Jewish women are sitting on the sidewalk in their beach chairs, gossiping and whispering about Carrie

Frances. Some of the women nod at Carrie Frances and smile. As Carrie Frances and Tracy pass Silstein Real Estate Office, the two men look out of the window at Carrie Frances.

Carrie Frances tells Tracy, "I don't know anyone in the neighborhood except my landlord's family. It's good to know someone else." Tracy asks, "Do you party?" Carrie Frances answers, "No." Tracy says, "Well, when I take care of this pregnancy, I am going to take you partying."

Carrie Frances replies softly, "I can't go dancing or anything. I am pregnant." Tracy doesn't answer but smiles at Carrie Frances as she goes into the laundromat. Tracy and little Blaine walk on to their house.

Later that day, Carrie Frances is back at her apartment. She hears a knock at her door. She is surprised to see Tracy and two small kids at her front door. As a matter of fact, she is really taken aback by this. Carrie Frances invites Tracy in and says, "It's nice to see you." Tracy, little Blaine, and his sister Nicky walk in. Looking around, Tracy says, "I love your apartment. This is beautiful. This is a bad M-F-ing apartment." Carrie Frances is taken aback by this and looks at Tracy and asks, "Would you like to have a seat? I'll make some tea."

Tracy and the kids sit at the kitchen table near the back door. Carrie Frances puts a teapot with water on the stove and set cups on the table with cheese, crackers, and cake. Tracy looks at the backyard and says, "I love your apartment; you have such a nice breeze with the air coming from front to back." Carrie Frances replies, "I like it too."

Carrie Frances pours tea for her and Tracy and juice and milk for Blaine and Nicky. Little baby Leena is sitting nearby in a carrying seat. Tracy, looking sad, says, "I am going to go to the hospital tomorrow. I'll be home tomorrow evening. Could you watch my kids? I know you won't hurt them. I realized that earlier when I met you." Carrie Frances thinks and says, "I don't mind, but give me all of your information about what hospital and your family for emergency. I just met you." Tracy replies, "All right." She writes down everything on a piece of paper and gives it to Carrie Frances. Carrie Frances tells Tracy, "Your kids can sleep in my bed and I'll sleep on the sofa." Tracy, with a serious look, says, "I hate to ask this of you, but I don't have anyone else. I am serious." Carrie Frances tells her, "I believe you."

The next day Tracy calls Carrie Frances and tells her that she is back from the hospital and she can bring the kids home. Shortly afterward Carrie Frances is at Tracy's door with her kids. When Tracy opens the door, Carrie Frances sees that Tracy is sick. She says, "Tracy, you are too sick to be home." Tracy says, "I had to come back to the kids. I sneaked off from the hospital. They wanted me to stay a couple of days. The last time I did this, I had this nurse give me one in her house. She went to work and left me, and I almost died. That's why I went to the hospital this time. The doctor said they were going to treat me with antibiotics; that's why they wanted to keep me in the hospital, and also I need to lie still." Carrie Frances tells her in a firm voice, "Get off your feet and go to bed."

Carrie Frances puts Leena down in her little carrying seat. Blaine and Nicky are happy to be home. Carrie Frances helps Tracy into bed. Carrie Frances tells Tracy that she needs antibiotics. Tracy tells her, "I stole some from the nurses' tray. It's only enough to last through the night."

Carrie Frances looks at the antibiotics. She takes one of the pills and puts it in a tissue, then puts the tissue in her pocket. She gives Tracy a pill with a glass of water. She tells Tracy, "I am going to my apartment to get some overnight clothes. You need someone to take care of you. I'll be back soon." Carrie Frances takes Leena and leaves.

Carrie Frances goes directly to her doctor's office up the block. She rings the bell. Her doctor opens the door and Carrie Frances goes in.

The doctor says, "Carrie Frances, did you decide to take care of your situation?" She replies softly, "No sir. My friend went and took care of herself at the hospital. They wanted her to stay a couple of days and treat her with antibiotics and get bed rest, but she sneaked out and came home. She wanted to be home with her kids. She's real sick. She stole enough antibiotics from the nurses' tray for the night. After that, she won't have any. I brought one of her pills with me." She pulls the tissue with the pill out and hands it to the doctor and asks, "Can you please give me a prescription so I can get her these pills."

He looks at Carrie Frances sadly and asks, "What's her name and where does she live?"

Carrie Frances tells him Tracy's name and address.

The doctor writes out the prescription and says, "I am giving you one for pain also. Tell her to come by here in a few days for a check-up. If she doesn't get better in a few days, call me and I'll do a house call. She's just down the block." Carrie Frances is so grateful and says, "Thanks so much."

On the way back Carrie Frances stops by the supermarket and buys lots of food for Tracy and her kids and has it delivered. She doesn't tell Tracy. She goes back to Tracy's house and tells her, "I got you some medicine." Tracy asks, "From where?" Carrie Frances explains everything to her.

"I took one of your pills and I went to the doctor down the street. I know him, so he gave me a prescription for your antibiotics and some pain pills. He said you should come to see him in a few days for a check-up. And, if you don't get better in a few days, you should call him, and he will make a house call. You're only a block and a half away." Tracy says, "Damn, you must really know him. Who paid for this?" Carrie Frances says, "I did."

The doorbell rings and Tracy wonders who it could be. Carrie Frances tells her that it's the food delivery. Tracy asks, "What food delivery?" She tells her, "I went by the supermarket." Tracy can't believe this—it's too good to be true—and says, "What?" Carrie Frances puts all the food away. Tracy looks so happy. She knows she has a true friend.

One year later at an after-hours club, Tracy is arguing with her boyfriend about money. Tracy picks up a chair and throws it at her boyfriend. Her boyfriend,

Gerald, slaps her. Tracy kicks Gerald. Gerald puts his hands around Tracy's neck and starts choking her. Carrie Frances sees and hears all of this and is upset and yells, "Stop! What are you doing? You trying to kill her?" Gerald takes his hands from around Tracy's neck. Out of breath, Tracy yells, "You better give me my f-ing money. I want it. You got a closet full of money." Pointing she says, "Look at all of those suitcases filled with money." Carrie Frances looks on, taking everything in, and says, "Tracy, I'll be out front by the bar. You all get it together." She looks at Gerald and says, "Please don't hurt her."

Carrie Frances walks out past the bar into the hallway and makes a phone call from the telephone booth. She is saying, "Yeah, come and pick me and my friend up. She and her boyfriend are arguing over money that he has in his office closet. He should just give her some so she can leave. Her boyfriend has an after-hours spot in the basement. The address is 15 East 46th Street, between Rutland Road and Midwood Street. Bring lots of your friends too. I am going to the bar to order a drink and wait for her."

Carrie Frances hangs up the telephone and goes back to the bar. She still hears Tracy arguing with Gerald. Carrie Frances goes into the office and says, "Tracy, let's go. You need to go home and see about your kids." Tracy is crying. Carrie Frances puts her arms around Tracy and leaves the room. Carrie Frances says, "Tracy, I am serious, let's go now. Everything will be all right." Tracy, wiping her eyes, says, "That SOB did me wrong."

A few minutes later Carrie Frances and Tracy walks out onto the street. They see several well-dressed men go into the club. Tracy looks at them and says, "They look like stone hustlers and white ones at that. I bet if one of them was my boyfriend, he'd give me money." Carrie Frances laughs and says, "Come on."

About thirty minutes later Carrie Frances and Tracy are at Carrie Frances's new apartment. The nanny, a middle-aged Italian lady, comes into the living room. She tells Carrie Frances, "You're home early." Smiling, she says, "Yeah, did anyone call?" The nanny smiles and says, "Yes, Irish Italian called." Tracy asks, "What does she mean?" Carrie Frances ignores Tracy's question and with a serious look asks, "Tracy, how much money was your boyfriend supposed to give you?" Tracy answers, "About fifty thousand dollars." Carrie Frances asks, "What were you going to do with it?" She replies happily, "Buy a co-op and a car." Carrie Frances replies, "Why not a house? If you had enough cash money to buy a house, a car, plus money to put in the bank, would you leave New York and live a nice comfortable life for you and your kids? And, also, stop messing with no-good men?" Tracy answers, "Yes, but where would I go." She tells her, "Where I am from, there are plenty of beautiful houses with lots of land for swimming pools, tennis courts, you name it. You could even open up a small business to keep you afloat without taking money from your bank account." Tracy says sadly, "If I had that kind of money, I would." Carrie Frances very seriously asks, "Are you serious?" Tracy replies, "Yes." She asks her, "Would you tell anyone where the money came from?" Tracy gives her a weird look and says, "No." Carrie Frances, with a serious look, says, "Are you positive?" She answers slowly and says, "Yes." Carrie Frances, more serious this time, says, "Are you sure, sure, sure?" Before Tracy can answer a knock is heard at the door.

The nanny answers the door in a happy voice and says, "Come in. Go on into the living room." Mr. Irish Italian is a handsome, six-foot, medium-build, well-dressed man. Two of Mr. Irish Italian's friends are with him but stay in the hallway of the apartment.

Mr. Irish Italian comes into the living room and says, "Hello, darling." Tracy looks shocked and says, "You look just like one of those men we saw going into the club." With a serious look he says, "No, you've never seen me before now." Carrie Frances gives Tracy a look that says shut up.

Carrie Frances and Mr. Irish Italian leave the living room and walk into the kitchen by the table. He asks her seriously, "Can you trust her?" Carrie Frances, a little upset, says, "We have to." He asks, "How much do you want to give her?" She asks him, "How much did you get?" He smiles and says, "We hit the jackpot." Carrie Frances tells him, "Give her three hundred thousand." He says, "Okay." He beckons for his two male friends to come into the kitchen and sit at the table.

The two men walk into the kitchen carrying suitcases. One friend is a little heavy set, mid-twenties, Irish man, about 6 foot, very handsome also. The other male is Afro American, the heaviest of the three, very well dressed and around 6 foot. The three men sit at the table and count the money. Mr. Irish Italian gives Carrie Frances money to give Tracy. He, also, gives Carrie Frances her share.

Carrie Frances goes back into the living room and talks to Tracy very seriously.

Tracy is a little scared. She doesn't know what is going on. Carrie Frances says, "Tracy, here's three hundred thousand. You are going to take this money and leave town. You are never to tell anyone when, where, or whom you got it from."

Nervously, Tracy asks, "Where am I going? I don't have anywhere to go." The three detectives stand back and listens with serious looks on their faces. Carrie Frances continues saying, "I have a place for you. The perfect state, the perfect town, the perfect house." She smiles and says, "Plenty of rooms, swimming pool, tennis court, and a lake. Those guys will be in jail for at least three days. Go home, pack your stuff, and don't even tell your family until much later about where you live. I'll get a U-Haul to take your things and my own drivers."

(End of Tracy's Flashback)

Tracy says, "I never looked back and here I am." She looks at Carrie Frances and says, "Carrie Frances, I want to know, was there ever a time that you were in need of somebody's help like we were?" Carrie Frances thinks for a while, smiles, and says, "Yeah, lots of times. I always called on God for help and I always got out of the situation." She pauses for a moment and continues, "Sometimes angels would come to my rescue. Tracy, right after you came from the hospital, I went through some tough times. Remember I told you that I had to move." Tracy replies, "Yeah, I remember that." Carrie Frances goes on to say, "It was real rough having an infant and pregnant again without a husband. I am not saying women can't take care of children on their own. If there is enough money and you are a good woman, you can do good by yourself and your kids. Back in those days people looked down on you if you had kids and no husband, especially if you were looking for an apartment."

Carrie Frances Flashback-Sept. 1974

Two well-dressed men, a little tipsy, approach Carrie Frances's basement apartment door. Dobby Shaw says, "Man, I want you to meet Carrie Frances. She's a nice girl and beautiful." He laughs and says, "She has the cutest little baby girl; her name is Leena." Terry C says, "Man, suppose her sister Mandolyn, your girlfriend, is not here." Dobby Shaw says, "Ah, don't worry, Carrie Frances will let me in. She knows I love playing with her baby. Man, she'll fix us food and even let us crash until tomorrow." He pauses and says, "Don't worry, she's not dating anybody, and she never goes anywhere." Dobby rings the doorbell, but no one answers.

Carrie Frances hears the doorbell, but she can't answer because her sister Mandolyn is sleeping on the sofa in the living room with Ish. Mandolyn hears the doorbell and tiptoes into the bedroom. She is scared and whispers, "Carrie Frances, that's Dobby and one of his friends. They just finished playing at the club,

Tempo Soul City. Dobby said he might stop by." Breathing heavy she says, "Ish and I will hide in the closet." Carrie Frances, upset, says to her, "How am I going to explain the sofa being unmade? You know he's going to want to come into the bedroom and look at Leena until she wakes up. That man loves that baby like he is her real uncle." Really upset she continues, "Why do you think he always wants you to bring her over to the radio station when you visit him and his friend Terry C?" Mandolyn, looking stupid, says, "You're right about that."

Ish is lying on the sofa afraid to move. Ish doesn't know what is going on. Dobby is still ringing the doorbell. Carrie Frances can hear them talking outside of the door. She also hears the landlord's door open from upstairs. Terry C realizes that Dobby is ringing the bell too much and says, "Dobby, bro, that's enough! She's not home, let's go." He looks up and sees the landlord, and says, "Oh my god, that's the landlord. Dobby let's go. I don't need any trouble." Dobby is angry and says, "Carrie Frances is in there. Mandolyn must be in there with another man, because Carrie Frances would answer her door." The landlord yells, "She must not be home. Why are you still ringing the bell?" Dobby angrily yells, "You m-----f----r, go back in the house and mind your business." Terry C drags Dobby away out of the gate.

The next day Carrie Frances's landlady is telling her the bad news. The landlady sadly says, "Carrie Frances, I know you are a good girl. That's why we rented the apartment to you. We knew you were young, with a newborn baby, and no husband. Seriously, I know those men came to see your sister and not you." Carrie Frances replies, "Yes, they did. My sister was here with another boyfriend. When Dobby and his friend stopped by last night, I couldn't let them in and have a fight in here. I didn't know Dobby would ring the doorbell so long and curse out Lacy."

The landlady says, "Well, Lacy said he didn't rent the apartment to your sister. He rented it to you. He also said you have three months to find another place to live. I am so sorry, but I can't do anything, because this is Lacy's house. If it was left up to me, I would let you stay, because I know that will never happen again."

A few days later Carrie Frances is walking past the Silstein Real Estate Office on East 51st Street and Clarkson Avenue. She sees a sign in the window for a three-and-a-half-room apartment for rent on East 91st Street and Clarkson Avenue, and thinks, Oh, there's an apartment for rent, but I need two bedrooms so the kids can have their own room. She buys a newspaper from the newsstand in hopes of finding an apartment. The next couple of days, Carrie Frances walks with baby Leena looking for an apartment. She rings doorbells and people slam doors in Carrie Frances's face. She walks with baby Leena in the rain, sleet and snow; she walks with baby Leena until she is exhausted.

About a month later Carrie Frances walks past the real estate office on her way to the laundromat. She does not see any apartment-for-rent signs in the window. She walks back from the laundromat, weary, crying and thinks, *Lord, I don't see an apartment-for-rent sign in the window, but maybe they have something that they haven't put up yet. I'll take whatever they have. Lord, suppose they don't accept me because I am a single mother. I don't have a husband.* She takes a deep breath. *I have a baby, I am pregnant, and I am still in my teens. Oh, God! You must help me.* Carrie Frances wipes the tears from her eyes. She gets the courage to walk into the real estate office, but very humble.

The two Silstein brothers are in the office. One brother is in the rear, holding a file, getting ready to put it in the file cabinet. The other brother is on the right, behind a desk with his back toward the window. As Carrie Frances enters, the brother behind the desk stands as if he has been waiting for her.

Carrie Frances says softly, "Excuse me. I was wondering if you have any apartments for rent." The first Silstein brother, standing and smiling, says, "Yes, Carrie Frances, for you, we do." The second Silstein brother in the rear almost drops his files but tries to keep a straight face. Carrie Frances is taken aback by this. The first Silstein brother excitedly says, "Carrie Frances, we know you. We've been watching you since you first moved in the neighborhood. We see you and your baby every day. We watch you from our window." Lying, she replies, "My husband is in the service." Both of the Silstein brothers know she doesn't have a husband. The first Silstein brother cuts her off and says, "We don't care about that. You're a decent girl. You carry yourself like an adult. We admire you. We have the perfect apartment for you. It's three and a half rooms on East Ninety-First Street and Clarkson Avenue, but I have to tell you, Carrie Frances, you'll be integrating this building. You'll be the first African American to move in there. We know you won't have a problem. We also know what happened with your present landlord." He smiles and says, "Carrie Frances, his loss is our gain." He leans over his desk and starts writing. "Here's the address. You go over there and meet the super and if he says you can have the apartment, it's yours. Also, we won't paint because we just painted, and the tenant stayed only two days. The apartment is clean. Now, after six months, if you like, we'll paint the apartment any color you like."

Carrie Frances, almost speechless, takes the paper. The first Silstein brother smiles at Carrie Frances graciously. At that moment she is so thankful, and she says to him in such an appreciative manner, "Thank you so much." Carrie Frances turns and walks out of the Realtors' office.

(End of Carrie Frances Flashback)

Carrie Frances continues talking to the girls. "You see, I've had my share. We've all had our share and there is always someone to help. You know, those two men were angels. They saved my life and my kids. If it wasn't for them; I could have ended up in a bad neighborhood. And, it's no telling what would have happened to us. I stayed there for quite a few years. When I got ready to move, they told me that I was the best tenant they ever had. Also, that if I was ever in need of an apartment, please look them up, because there will always be an apartment for me in their buildings."

Tracy says to Carrie Frances, "I didn't know you went through all of that." Carrie Frances replies, "I know, I didn't tell you about it. You had your problems. I just tried to make my life better. I went back to work on Wall Street after I had my son. I realized something from that situation. You need a job in order to get certain things. No matter how much money you have, sometimes you have to show proof of employment to get in the door." She looks at Verlie and says, "Verlie and I both worked on Wall Street. That's where we met." Teri, smiling, says, "I am enjoying myself." Verlie replies, "We are all still standing strong." Baby Doll says, "And we are going to stay like that."

The Unholy Five Queens toast each other. After the toast, they get on the dance floor and put everybody to shame dancing.

6

OLD COUNTRY STORE WITH CONFEDERATE FLAG

Carrie Frances walks into the old country store. She gets lots of cinnamon buns, honey buns, cheese doodles and pork skins. Two tipsy Caucasian old-timers are sitting in the store looking on. One of the old-timers is a little tipsier than the other one and has a whiskey bottle in a brown paper bag. The other old-timer pretends not to be tipsy. A young Asian man with blond hair is putting things away in the store. The old-timer store owner is behind the counter. He looks as if he's happy to see Carrie Frances without anyone noticing. Carrie Frances goes to the counter.

The old man says, "Well, it's nice for you to stop in again and buy all of these buns." He smiles and says, "I guess you'll be needing to fill up with some gas."

Carrie Frances nods, smiles, and says, "Yes, sir, I reckon so."

She goes into her purse and hands the man some money. The man rings up the items, but you see that he gives Carrie Frances the same amount of money back as her change. He says to the Asian man, "Bubby, come take these bags out to the car for the lady." Bubby replies, "Okay, Grandpa."

Bubby takes Carrie Frances's bags to the car. The old man leaves from behind the counter and walks out of the store behind Carrie Frances. When they get outside, they have a conversation.

The old man says, "It's so nice to see you. You're looking good as usual." He looks at Bubby and says, "This is my grandson. He's the only grandchild I have." Carrie Frances looks at Bubby, smiles, and says, "He's a fine young man. I know you are proud of him." The old man replies, "I am."

Carrie Frances looks as if she wants to hug both of them but doesn't. She gets into the car and says, "I'll see you the next time I come through. Thanks a lot for everything." The old man says to her, "No! I thank you." Carrie Frances drives away slowly, forcing a smile because she really feels like crying.

Bubby looks at his grandpa. The old man has tears in his eyes and says, "Bubby, did you get a good look at that lady? You need to remember her face." Bubby, with a curious look, says, "Grandpa! Why? Who is she?" The old man replies, "Let's go over here and sit. It's time that I tell you something."

The old man sits down on a bench outside of the store. Bubby sits with him looking halfway scared. The old man says, "Bubby, I am getting old now. There is something you need to know, cause your momma, Patti Cake, might not ever tell you." Bubby looks at his

Grandpa and asks, "What, Grandpa?" He replies, "First of all, I don't charge that lady for anything she gets from this store, even the gas that I put in her car." Bubby asks, "Why not?" The old man continues, "First of all her name is Carrie Frances and that lady, when she was just a teenager, she saved you and your momma, Patti Cake's lives." Bubby, with a curious look, asks, "How?"

The old man goes on to say, "Well, Carrie Frances grew up around here. I knew her father. We used to fish together. Patti Cake and Carrie Frances were good friends and another little girl named Baby Doll. When they got up some size about sixteen or seventeen years old, they left here together two days after graduation. Well, your momma, Patti Cake, called occasionally and then we didn't hear from her for a long time. Then she called and said she was fine. So, two and a half years later, early one morning before daybreak, a car pulled up. I couldn't imagine who it could be."

Patti Cake Flashback-Nov. 1975

"There was a knock at the door. I opened it and there stood Carrie Frances holding you in her arms and holding onto your momma, Patti Cake. By that time your grandma Jolie was up. Carrie Frances said, 'Mr. Cal, don't worry, she's all right. She's just tired and needs rest.'" He looked at Bubby and said, "Your momma, Patti Cake, had on a nightgown and bedroom slippers and that was it. You were in a little gown with bare feet. Carrie Frances had clothes on." The old man shakes his head and continues, "I didn't know what to think. Your momma was so glad to be home. Your grandma put her in bed and you beside her." The old man's eyes are tearing. "Your momma looked at me and your grandma and said some words I'll never forget. Patti Cake in a soft voice said, 'Momma, Daddy, aren't you going to kiss me.' I said, 'Of course, Patti Cake. I am glad you are home. You and my grandchild.' I leaned over and kissed Patti Cake, and your grandma Jolie leaned over and kissed her too. Carrie Frances said, 'Mr. Cal, I have to get my kids from the car and some luggage. Could you help me, please?'" The old man, still sitting in front of the store, takes a deep sigh and continues talking to his grandson.

"Bubby, when I got to the front of the passenger side of the car, there was a baby sleeping on the floor of the car on a quilt and another one about a year old in the passenger seat asleep. There was a blanket in the backseat; I guess Patti Cake used that for cover to keep her warm, being that she didn't have on nothing but her night clothes. There was also a quilt on the floor of the backseat too. I reckon Patti Cake must have let you sleep there, so she wouldn't drop you while she was sleeping. There were three large suitcases in the trunk and a shopping bag with papers and files. When we got back in the house, I got a good look at you children. You looked like a little China baby. Carrie Frances's little baby looked like a little chocolate teddy bear. The older one looked like a little white baby with blue eyes and blonde hair. Her hair was braided with lots of grease and on the ends of each braid, Carrie Frances had tiny little rubber bands to keep her hair from coming loose. Bubby, while looking at Carrie

Frances's older baby, I said to myself, 'This must be Patti Cake's baby'. Carrie Frances saw me looking at her baby and said, 'Mr. Cal, these two are my kids. Patti Cake only has one baby and he's a week old.' Carrie Frances pointed to the shopping bag and said, 'Mr. Cal, those are Patti Cake's papers. And we need to open these suitcases.' Carrie Frances looked at me and your grandma Jolie and said, 'Mr. Cal, Mrs. Jolie, you don't have to worry. No one is after us. We just had to leave in a hurry. I made it in seven hours. I only stopped for gas twice.' Bubby, I was shocked at seeing all of that money. So, I said, 'Carrie Frances, are you sure nobody is after you two?' Carrie Frances smiled and with a serious tone said, 'I am positive no one is after us.'" The old man sighs and continues telling the story.

"A few days later, Carrie Frances and Patti Cake paid down on this store here. The man who owned it said he would take half and I could pay the balance off later. There was enough money to pay for it at one time, but Carrie Frances said it was a good idea not to let people know we had that much money. Carrie Frances got a lawyer to handle the buying of the store. The man who owned the store changed his mind and said he didn't want to sell it to me." The old man takes another deep sigh, looks at his grandson, and continues telling the story.

"Carrie Frances went off for a couple of hours and came back. All of a sudden, Carrie Frances pulled up in this same yard here. Then another car pulled up with three guys. A young white guy was driving. You could tell he had money by the way he was dressed. He had on a gold Rolex, with a thick gold chain around his neck, and diamond rings on his fingers. When he walked, you knew he meant business. He looked humble, but yet, you could see the fire in his eyes that he would kill you and wouldn't think twice about it. There were two guys with him, one was a heavy-set black guy and a medium size white guy. They were dressed the same and had the same fire in their eyes. Carrie Frances stood off on the side near the store. From the looks of the long coat she was wearing, it seemed as if she might have had a shotgun underneath it. She had a stand and a look I had never seen in her before. I do believe she would have killed that man too and wouldn't have thought about it afterward." The old man seems to be getting tired but continues telling his grandson the story.

"Well, the first guy walked over to the man who owned the store and they talked for a little while. I don't know what he said to him, but that man signed those papers and took the balance of the money right on the spot. All of a sudden, the lawyer showed up and finalized the papers on the spot. I felt sorry for the man who sold me the store. He looked at me and looked up at that old Confederate flag, pointing, and said, 'That flag there shows a lot of people their way.' I knew he was telling me in his own way that he would like for the flag to stay up." (End of Patti Cake Flashback)

Mr. Cal continues his conversation with Bubby. "I am not what that flag stands for, but a lot of people come in here and say, 'I thought I was lost until I saw this store with the flag, and I knew I was going in the right direction.' Bubby, even though the flag might show some people their way, it's time for it to come down, now.

Those three guys left from here that day and I haven't seen them since. But a few years later, I was down at the beach, buying some fresh fish for the store. Me and old Jerold in there passed this nice restaurant, where they had nice tables outside to eat. And I know for a fact that it was those same three guys I saw walking into that restaurant. They looked as if they owned the place by the way the patrons were treating them as they walked in. The name of the restaurant was Irish Italian. I didn't say anything to Jerold about it. Bubby, no one knows about anything I am telling you except your grandma Jolie, your momma, Patti Cake and Carrie Frances, and I want you to keep it that way, you hear?" Bubby asks, "Grandpa is that how we got the house we live in?" The old man answers, "Yep, we used to live in an old shack back down the road."

The old man looks at Bubby and shakes his head with exhaustion and continues the story. "That same day that those three guys came and made that man sell me this store, well, Carrie Frances had a builder named Bingham from up there by Chester to come that same day. He had a blueprint already laid out. He built this house in four months. Carrie Frances told me to put these fences on the front and on each side of the store and also on the side of the road so nobody could see how big and pretty the house really was. That would keep people out of our business. That's why the pine trees were planted in front of the house and over on the side, so you couldn't see the swimming pool and tennis court.

Boy, you have a mansion here. We only spent half of the money. I found out later that Carrie Frances drew the blueprint for this here house. Carrie Frances's brother was a builder in another state. She is very smart." The old man looks around, shakes his head and smiles, and continues telling his grandson the story.

"Until this day, nobody ever came looking for Carrie Frances and Patti Cake. I never asked Patti Cake why she only had her gown on. I believe they were in such a hurry that they had to leave then or never, and grab what was important, which was you and the money. You see, Bubby, Carrie Frances is family. She looked out for your momma."

The old man looks at Bubby and says, "There's more." Bubby replies, "Really!" The old man spits, and says, "Yep, some months later, Patti Cake went to secretarial school and got a job working at the motel. Then she started to run with the owner's son. Then one weekend, Carrie Frances came home and the next thing you know, your momma, Patti Cake had taken up with the owner and a few days later they got married. Now the owner is dead and your momma, Patti Cake owns the motel." The old man looks at Bubby again and continues, "Now, don't you go and tell your momma, Patti Cake, that I told you all of this. I just want you to know this in case Patti Cake never tells you. Now if she does tell you on her own, pretend you are surprised."

While the old man and Bubby are outside finishing their talk, the old-timers are inside of the store, wondering why it's taking them so long. So, they have their own conversation about what's going on. Old-Timer Jerold, tipsy and upset, says, "You see, he's been out there for a long time. I tell you, there is something going on with Cal and that girl." He shakes his head and continues, "She's been coming through here for years." Old-Timer Drunk, holding his bottle of whiskey, says, "Shut up! Mind your own business." Old-Timer Jerold, still upset, says, "I am telling you, something's been up with them. He gives her money back to her. I see it with my own eyes." Old-Timer Drunk, shaking his head, says, "Liar, stop talking about my friend."

The old man and his grandson, Bubby, get up and walk back into the store carrying the Old Confederate Flag.

7

A LOT'S GOING ON TODAY

Carrie Frances is back from the old country store. She and Orchard are in the kitchen talking. She's telling him that she doesn't want to go to a funeral on New Year's Day. Therefore, she should go and view Billy C at the funeral parlor. Orchard tells her that he'll drive her. She's happy to hear that and says, "All right."

Orchard looks at the bags of goodies, laughs, and asks, "What are you going to do with all of these buns?" She laughs and says, "Have some good old time eating. You should see all of the other stuff. Look, I've got pork rinds, Blenheim Ginger Ale, cheese doodles, and my favorite old-fashion cookies. Oh, by the way, I am going out to the country house later and burn some of those old papers and clothes that's in the shed." He replies, "That'll be good. You've been planning to do that for a long time." Carrie Frances looks at the clock on the wall and says, "Um, it's eleven o'clock. I think we better go on to the funeral parlor because I have a lot to do today." Orchard gets up and goes out to the truck to wait for Carrie Frances. As soon as he is out of the door, she gets her cell phone and sends a text. A reply text comes back and she smiles, gets her purse, and goes out the door.

Good Old Times Again

There is a lot going on in a nearby motel in North Carolina. Believe it or not, there are two old ladies sticking up a male motel manager. Both of the old ladies have guns with silencers drawn. He can't believe he's being jacked by these old ladies. He's giving them all of his money and putting it into a large green garbage bag. One old lady takes the green garbage bag and puts it into a large suitcase, while the other old lady continues to have her gun drawn on the manager. The old lady with the suitcase takes a small can of spray from her coat pocket and sprays the manager's face and leaves calmly. The other old lady points the gun at the right side of the manager's head, but then shoots him in his left shoulder and leaves calmly also.

Simultaneously, in another part of the same motel, two more old ladies, wearing coats, hats, gloves and each carrying a shoulder bag, are in a room with a maid. Each of the old ladies has a gun drawn with a silencer. They make the maid lie down on her back in the bed with her knees up. One old lady points the gun to the right side of her head, while the other old lady pulls out a small can of spray and sprays the maid's face. The old lady put the spray can back in her pocket while still holding her gun on the maid. The one holding the gun to the right side of the maid's head, then points to her right shoulder and shoots; and the other old lady shoots the maid in her left foot. They each shoot simultaneously, and put their guns in their purses, and walks out of the room; They put the Do Not Disturb sign on the doorknob and calmly walk away.

Saying Goodbye

Thirty minutes later Carrie Frances and Orchard are at the funeral parlor viewing Billy C's body. She cries uncontrollably. Orchard comforts her. She stands over him reflecting on all of the good times that they shared. She realizes that this is the last time she'll ever be able to be this close to him. Even if she goes to the funeral, she won't be able to spend this much time in privacy as she can now. So, she is making the best of this last viewing.

As they are leaving, Carrie Frances asks Orchard to stop her by the supermarket. Orchard waits in the truck while she goes in and shops. It doesn't take her much time at all to get what she wants, and they are off to her house. On the ride back, Orchard tries to make conversation to keep her from thinking of Billy C. Once Orchard drops Carrie Frances off and pulls out of her driveway, she takes her packages into the house, puts things away, gets into her car, and drives off.

A half hour later, Carrie Frances is driving into the parking lot of the Palmetto Motel. She sees the Unholy Four exiting a Ford Taurus in the parking lot. Verlie is exiting the driver's seat. They get shopping bags from Walmart out of the trunk. Verlie picks up a shopping bag with Christmas wrapping paper sticking out of it. The four of them goes into the motel. Carrie Frances doesn't say anything to them, because they are unaware of her being in the parking lot.

Carrie Frances goes into the nearby restaurant and orders lunch. An hour and a half later as Carrie Frances is exiting the restaurant, she sees the Unholy Four getting into their individual cars. Verlie gets into her pimped-up 1968 GTO. Teri gets into her BMW. Tracy gets into a Mercedes-Benz, and Baby Doll gets into her Jaguar. They all drive off in different directions. Carrie Frances sees this but doesn't give them a second look and walks over toward the motel. Twenty minutes later, Carrie Frances is coming out of the motel room with the same two pieces of luggage that she carried into the motel room a day earlier. She gets into her car and drives away.

Burn, Baby, Burn

A half hour later Carrie Frances is in the backyard of her farmhouse. She takes old bags of clothes from a nearby shed and puts them into two already burning barrels. She walks to the trunk of her car and opens it. She opens the small suitcase in the trunk and removes two medium-size, beautifully wrapped gifts and puts them into a beautiful Christmas bag. She closes the small suitcase and opens the large one and removes four large Walmart shopping bags. She closes the trunk and walks back to the backyard with the four bags.

She takes things out of the large bags and puts them into the burning barrels. She takes out some old coats, shoes, gloves, and wigs and drops them into the burning flames of the barrels. She goes back to the shed and gets more old clothes and puts them on top of the burning flames. She goes back and gets another bag full of clothes and closes the shed door. Carrie Frances puts the bag of clothes near the burning barrels. She goes over and sits on the back doorstep and watches the flames burn. She has a far-off look on her face. After sitting for a few minutes, she goes over to the barrels, picks up a nearby stick, and stirs the flames to make sure that everything is burning. She returns to the doorstep and sits.

Suddenly, she gets up and goes to the gate a few feet behind the burning barrels and opens it. She goes into this covered gate, and suddenly, music can be heard. She comes out from the covered gate and puts more old clothes into the burning flames. Carrie Frances begins to dance around the barrels as if she's celebrating. She hears her cell phone ringing and she answers it. It's Patti Cake, who asks, "Are you finished with everything?" Carrie Frances says, "Yes, I am finished with everything. It's all done. Thanks so much." Patti Cake replies, "Okay, talk later."

Carrie Frances has something on her mind. It has been burning in her mind for years and she has to do something about it. As a matter of fact, it has been burning since her early childhood when she first heard her uncle speak about it. Through the years it was as if by fate that everything was put into motion. It was as if she was the savior of so many people. So therefore, it's her duty and destiny to make it right for everyone concerned. Time waits for no one. Whatever a person wants to do, they better do it fast so they can enjoy it. Patti Cake is a dear friend of Carrie Frances, and pretty much everything she owns is because of Carrie Frances. What she is about to tell Patti Cake might break up their friendship. She knows Patti Cake is a good girl and will be thankful for the information and will do what she is supposed to and should do. If Patti Cake decides not to do what is right, Carrie Frances knows that she did the right thing by telling her and her conscience will be clean. Everyone has a destiny. Angels are all around to help you reach it. This task was given to her many years ago to fulfil and it has now reached full fruition. It's now or never.

Destiny

Carrie Frances says, "Patti Cake, don't hang up. I want to talk to you about something." She replies, "All right, what is it?" Carrie Frances says, "I went by your father's store today and I saw Bubby. I think you should tell him about what happened, sooner than later. You know your father is getting old now and sometimes people like to get things off their chest. I think it's best that he hears it from you, or at least soon after he hears it from someone else." Patti Cake replies, "You know, I've been thinking about that myself. I think he will understand." Carrie Frances replies, "Of course he will, you are his mother. And you have been a good mother. He'll be very appreciative of you telling him." Patti Cake then says, "Carrie Frances, there has been something that I've been intending to ask you for years. I just got so caught up with Jack and everything." She pauses for a second and asks, "Why did you tell me to leave Jack Junior and get involved with Jack Senior?" When Carrie Frances hears this, it's like God himself is there. This is exactly what she wanted to talk to Patti Cake about and tell her things that she didn't know about her husband, Jack Senior, and also to explain her part in it.

Carrie Frances takes a deep sigh and replies, "I am happy you asked me that. I knew at that point of Jack Junior's life he would not have married you. He just wanted someone to play around with. He also wanted his father's approval. That meant bringing home someone with old money and a beauty queen. Now, beauty queen you were and still are. But old money you didn't have. And, also, you did not need to tell him about the money we came home with."

Carrie Frances takes a deep breath and continues, "Now, at that point of Jack Senior's life, he was old, rich, flamboyant, and enjoyed taking a walk on the wild side. A matter of fact he has been taking a walk on the wild side since before he was Jack Junior's age. And, also, he had an ego as big as we are from California and back. And that ego would get bigger just by taking his son's girl. Also, proving to you that he could love you and do more for you than Jack Junior could by marrying you and giving you everything that he had. And that's exactly what he did.

He married you three days after you slept with him. And look where you are now. You own the resort and much, much more. You have enough money to live fifty lifetimes in style and still have money left over. Jack

Junior wouldn't do that because he was afraid to stand up to his father, because in his eyes you were not good enough for him and didn't pass his father's test. Jack Senior was slick. You passed the test for him, but not for his son. But it worked in your favor. I knew this and that's another reason I insisted that you get with Jack Senior; And most importantly, I wanted you to settle down to a stable lifestyle. I didn't ever want you to go back to what you went through in New York. I wasn't about to let you lose all of what you had at your fingertips by choosing the wrong man. Patti Cake, are you angry at me?" Patti Cake is taking it very well and replies, "No, Carrie Frances, I am not angry at you. I love you and you've never misled me. You've gotten me out of situations that I wouldn't have been able to get out of by myself." She pauses a second and continues, "I am a filthy, filthy rich woman because of you." Then she laughs and says, "I am a high-society girl now. Tell me what you meant by Jack Senior has been walking on the wild side since he was Jack Junior's age?"

Carrie Frances walks over to the barrels and puts more old clothes on the dying flames and takes a deep breath. "Well, I don't know if you know it or not, but it's about the land that the resort is on. You know it's leased land, right?" She replies, "Yes, I know it's leased for ninety-nine years. The lease will be up in 2055." Carrie Frances asks, "Do you know who it is leased from and how much money was paid to lease it?" Hearing this really gets Patti Cake's attention, and she says, "Carrie Frances, what are you trying to tell me? You know you can tell me anything. I looked for those lease agreement papers; I even asked our lawyer about them. He told me not to worry about them and he would give them to me when the time comes."

Carrie Frances is now sitting on the back doorstep again, still talking on the cell phone. She says, "Patti Cake, back in 1956, Jack Senior seduced a black woman around his age. She owned all of the land that the resort is on, plus the surrounding land. Jack Senior wanted her to sign the land over to him, but she refused when she found out what he was up to. But Jack Senior had taken precautions and had a backup plan. Prior to that, he had taken pictures of the two of them in very compromising positions. He also had pictures of her with his best friend in the same compromising way. He seduced her from his friend just so he could get the land.

Jack Senior gave her a thousand dollars for the entire ninety-nine years and nothing else. The lady was too embarrassed to try to take him to court. She was also a church lady and back in those times people didn't mix together as they do now. The old lady used to work as a cook at that restaurant on number eight on the right side, just before the intersection. If you look hard, you just might find those pictures. Patti Cake, are you there?" Patti Cake is in shock and is very quiet for a while. Finally, she says, "Wow! Carrie Frances, why didn't you tell me that then?" Carrie Frances replies, "I didn't want you to take your eyes and mind off where you were going and what you had to do to get there." Patti Cake, digesting everything, says, "I have to find her and give her money for all of those years she got nothing. I can imagine she's heartbroken about the double cross. Everybody makes mistakes when they are young. Look at me." Carrie Frances breathes a sigh of relief and says, "Yes, we all do make mistakes. Each of us is entitled to forgiveness also. I am quite sure that old lady will be happy to get her money. For all we know, she might be barely getting by. Patti Cake, it's so nice of you to make amends of this situation."

Patti Cake, in a sad voice, says, "Carrie Frances, I forgot to ask, how are you holding up with your loss of Billy C?" She replies with a smile and says, "Patti Cake, it's funny, but I feel so sad sometimes, but in a way, I feel free for the first time in a long time." She looks at the burning barrels and continues talking.

"You know, I felt guilty for running away. I've been feeling guilty since his death. I keep thinking, had I not run away and stayed and married him, he might be alive now. But, then, how do I know what would have happened? I was sitting here before you called, and I felt free for the first time since we left home. It's weird, but I feel free to do anything, to love, to do whatever. And this time around, I won't make mistakes as I did in the past. Patti Cake, do you realize that both of us are free?" She replies, "Not until you just mentioned it. Girl, we are free." Laughing, she continues, "And we are still young and beautiful." Carrie Frances, laughing also, says, "Yes, we are! We are queens now, not little princesses. Our kids are princesses and princes. We are young and old enough to know how to really enjoy life without mistakes."

While talking on the phone with Carrie Frances,

Patti Cake has been very busy. After hearing all of this information, Patti Cake has been sitting at her desk and has written out a check for $1.5 million. Patti Cake replies, "Well, my best girlfriend, I thank you for everything. I am going to make somebody very happy. It might be too late for Christmas, but it's not too late for New Year's." Carrie Frances is still sitting on the back doorstep. She replies happily with teary eyes, "Yes, she will be happy. Thanks, Patti Cake. I love you with all my heart. And here's to a New Year and the rest of our lives of being happy and free. Talk soon." Patti Cake says, "Happy New Year to you, too. Talk soon."

Carrie Frances closes her cell phone, walks over to the low burning flames, and dumps all of the clothes and the bag into the barrel. The burning flames become strong and bright.

Carrie Frances goes back into the covered gate. This time you can see the beauty of this hidden garden. A marble dance floor with beautiful tables and chairs on each side. An outdoor kitchen, a jukebox, and beautiful plants are everywhere. As you look further into the garden, you see a large swimming pool, a tennis court, and a jacuzzi. You can see a pool house connected to a three-car garage. It's a hidden oasis.

Carrie Frances goes over to the garage and opens it, revealing a money-green Rolls-Royce, an old 1969 pimped-up Mustang convertible, and also a 1975 sky blue Cadillac.

Carrie Frances comes back to the dance floor and starts dancing to the music almost trance-like. You can see the flames from the blazing fire from the barrels.

She dances over to a pole in the center of the dance floor and begins to swing on the pole.

Unbeknownst to Carrie Frances, but at this very moment as she dances, something good is going on in the next county. Preparation is being made for the greatest New Year's Eve surprise for an old lady. This time tomorrow that old lady will have everything that is rightfully hers. The old lady's prayers have been answered. Carrie Frances feels something deep in her heart and soul as she dances. Truthfully, she sees it in her mind's eye exactly as it will be this very moment as she dances.

At Last

It is New Year's Eve and a limousine pulls up to an old house as an old gray-haired black lady is sweeping the porch. The limousine driver opens the door. Patti Cake steps out with a Christmas shopping bag. The old lady looks hard through her thick glasses. She knows this is Mrs. Patti Shriver. Patti Cake takes the short, long walk to the porch. The old lady is shocked and has hurt in her eyes and says, "Hello! What can I do for you?" Patti Cake takes a deep breath with tears in her eyes and says, "I have something that I think belongs to you." She pauses and says, "I just found out from a dear girlfriend of mine late yesterday evening about the situation between you and my late husband. I brought you a gift." Pulling out the envelope, she continues, "And here's a check for 1,500,000 dollars."

The old lady is standing with her mouth open, speechless, with tears in her eyes. Mrs. Patti Shriver, a little more composed, says, "I also put ten thousand dollars cash in the envelope. I didn't know your dress size, so I bought you a robe and a bottle of perfume." She looks at the old lady and says, "I am so sorry for what happened. Please forgive my husband."

The old lady, more composed also, looks at Patti and says, "It was the Lord. I've prayed every hour, every day, and every year since that happened." The old lady takes the envelope and bag and says, "Wait here." The old lady walks back into her shack and comes back holding a worn Saint James Bible next to her chest with the envelope on top of the Bible in one hand and the shopping bag in the other hand. She kisses the Bible and says, "I have to accept this in the name of the Lord because I know it was by his grace that this miraculous blessing happened. Ever since that situation between your husband and me, I promised the Lord that when I got paid for my land, I would accept it in his name." She looks at the Bible and says, "I accept this in the name of the Lord, and I forgive you and your husband in the name of the Lord."

She looks at Patti and says, "You said your girlfriend told you about me." Mrs. Patti Shriver looks at the old lady and answers, "Yes, she told me late yesterday evening." She laughs and continues, "I guess the Lord let her hear your prayers." Patti thinks to herself and says, "You know, she's both of our angels. I'll let you in on a little secret." Her eyes tearing, she says, "She saved my baby's life and mine many years ago. We've been friends since childhood." The old lady puts down the shopping bag and puts her arms around

Mrs. Patti Shriver, and gives her the biggest, warmest hug and says, "Now, don't think about this anymore. You've done what the Lord wanted you to do. Just go on and enjoy your life and take care of yourself and your child, and if you see me in passing, say hello or give me a wave." She looks at Patti and says, "And please say thanks to your girlfriend. I'll have both of you in my prayers always."

Mrs. Patti Shriver walks back to the limousine. The driver opens the door and Patti gets into the limousine. The driver gets back into the driver's seat and turns the limousine around and drives away. The old lady goes back into her old shack.

8

NEW YEAR'S EVE CELEBRATION

Carrie Frances is finishing up a phone conversation with a big smile on her face. "Thanks, Patti, I knew everything would turn out all right." She comes back and joins in with Viola, Maggie Mae, and Cousin Caleb, who are sitting around in the living room. They are eating and drinking, and all dressed up to bring the New Year in. Carrie Frances has the best assortment of food. There's expensive wine, champagne, sodas, juices, and eggnog to drink. Everybody is happy and Carrie Frances says, "It feels so nice to be bringing the New Year in with my two favorite cousins and my best buddy. You know, I have never attended a funeral on New Year's." Viola says, "Me neither. I am not going to the funeral. I can't take it. I never liked going to funerals. Reen used to make me go to all of those funerals when I was little. Now that I got the pressure, I can't take it." Maggie Mae puts her words in and says, "Well, I am sho going. There ain't nothing else to do around here.

I have a good time at funerals. You see everybody. Everybody you ain't seen in a long time. You wear your best clothes, fix your hair all nice; Might even catch a man." Cousin Caleb adds to the conversation, "Cusin, I gon too. I am gon put ma best suit on. I be sharp as a tac, you'll shee. I won't be yookin for no woman 'cause I got ma Cat at home. But, I sho be yookin at the people and talking." Carrie Frances continues, "Well, I have no choice, I have to go. He was almost my husband." She smiles and says, "Cousin Caleb, your cousin here will be styling in her leopard dress, with pearls and diamonds." Viola goes on to say, "Carrie Frances, Ola Jean and Loletha show out over their dead. They cry so much, until they faint. People have to carry them out. I mean they fall on the floor and kick." Carrie Frances with a serious look says, "I hope they don't do that tomorrow. Maggie Mae, if I start crying, I want you and Caleb to help me. I don't want to cry so much that my eyes get swollen, and my lipstick smears, and I'll be looking all ugly. You know me, I want to look beautiful at all times." Cousin Caleb says, "Cusin Ker Francie, Maggie Mae and I will be there for you." Carrie Frances replies, "I know you will, Caleb, you and Maggie Mae. Let's have a drink. Caleb, you and I will have eggnog. Viola, you and Maggie Mae have some of this Moet. A client gave me this Moet when I was doing a musical in New York fourteen years ago for New Year's."

Maggie Mae interrupts and says, "Oh, guess whut I heard? I heard that yesterday, over yonder in North Carolina. Four old, old women robbed the motel and beat up the manager and a maid. Some people say they shot them wit' a gun that didn't make no noise. And they say that manager and the maid didn't want nobody to call the po-lice. I ain't never heard nothing like that. I wonder why they didn't want no po-lice to know they got the mess kicked out of 'em." Cousin Caleb says, "Yeah, I hurd the same ting myself." Viola says, "I didn't hear that. I guess somebody will call and tell me or I can find out by reading *The Darlboro Herald* News Paper." Maggie Mae says, happily, "I am Miss *Darlboro Herald*. I know everything that happens around here." Everyone laughs and Carrie Frances says, "Um, things are getting bad down here. They must have done it late at night." Maggie Mae says, "No gurl, it was between 11 and 11:30 in the morning. Broad daylight! I am serious, it sho nuff was." Carrie Frances said, "Um, that's the time Orchard and I went to view Billy C's body. Oh well, let's get on with our celebration."

Carrie Frances pours everybody drinks. They laugh and dance around. Suddenly, Carrie Frances breaks down crying and says, "Viola, I didn't get the chance to show him my name." Viola comforts Carrie Frances and takes her to the guest bedroom. As Carrie Frances lies on the bed in her guest bedroom, Viola sits on the right side of the bed rubbing her head and tells her, "Carrie Frances, everything will be all right. You'll get over this soon. You have to try to get your mind on something else. I don't want you to get sick. I know it's hard not to think about Billy C, but please try."

John the Baptist

Viola thinks for a second and looks at Carrie Frances and says, "Carrie Frances, about your dreams, when did you start having them? I know you told me, but I forgot. They always come true. I remember when we were in school you used to tell me about them." Carrie Frances looks at Viola and says, "Our old house sat on medium-height pillars. My sister Mandolyn and I used to play underneath the house. When the sun came up at that old house you could see the sun between the gap in the trees." With a far-off look she continues.

"When I was about nine years old, I had this dream about John the Baptist. I was playing underneath the house and John the Baptist, wearing a medium dark blue robe, with olive skin and curly-wavy hair, flew in from the east between that gap in the trees. I could feel and hear the wind as he flew in from the east and landed on my left side underneath the house. A Bible opened in front of me from the wind that was blowing as he flew in. The wind blew the pages instantly to a specific page. John the Baptist, looking at the page in the Bible, said to me, 'Recite this and you are saved.' I was afraid that I couldn't recite it, but I did recite it immediately and I was surprised. John the Baptist looked at me and said, 'You are saved.' I looked at the page in the Bible that I had just recited, and I saw a word, the word was written in the center of the page three times: at the top, middle, and bottom of the page in big letters. The word was '**FLAWLESS**.' From then on, I began to have true dreams." Viola, shaking her head, replies,

"That's amazing. The Lord gave you a wonderful gift at such an early age." Carrie Frances replies, "Yes, he sure did!"

Maggie Mae and Caleb are still in the living room enjoying themselves eating and drinking. Carrie Frances is happy about this because she remembers something that she wants to tell Viola without anyone else hearing. She pauses and looks at Viola with a strange look and says, "Viola, there is something that I've been wanting to tell you, but I kept forgetting it. As a matter of fact, I thought of it the night my god brother called and also the night that I called Billy C." Viola knows Carrie Frances is serious and sits up straight and says, "Okay, Carrie Frances! What is it?" She replies in a whispering voice, "I don't want Maggie Mae and Caleb to hear, so you must promise not to laugh when I tell you." Viola promises her that she will not laugh regardless of how funny it is.

Carrie Frances tells her that it's about the identical twin lookalike she saw of her when they were in the sixth grade. Viola's eyes are wide as if she can't believe what she is hearing. Carrie Frances says, "Yes, the girl you told me you saw that night at the ball game who looked identical to me." Viola says in a low voice, "What?" Carrie Frances replies, "Yes, that's the one. I've told some of my friends about this story several times and I am going to tell you the story again the way I told them because there have been nine encounters with this woman. I am very serious about this, Viola!" Viola says, "Go on, Carrie Frances, tell me the story. I promise, I won't laugh."

9 ENCOUNTERS IDENTICAL TWINS LOOKALIKE

1 Encounter:

When I was in the sixth grade there was a basketball game at school one night. Normally, Daddy would take me because he loved watching the games. As a matter of fact, he loved going to the games more than any of the other parents did.

I can even remember my daddy taking me to watch the games when my older brother was playing basketball in high school in an open outdoor court with his friends. My daddy would put me on his shoulders so I could see the games. I was about two years old, but I remember. I think that's probably why I love basketball to this day.

On this particular day I asked my father if he was taking me to the basketball game tonight and he replied, "No, I am not driving you to the game tonight." When I arrived at school later that morning my best friend, Viola, asked me if I was coming to the ballgame tonight. I told her no, and what my daddy had said to me earlier.

The following morning when I arrived at school, this is what Viola told me: "Carrie Frances, last night at the ballgame, I went into the girls' bathroom to fix my hair. I saw you standing there in front of me, looking in the mirror, fixing your hair too. I couldn't believe you were standing there and didn't speak to me. So, I said, 'Carrie Frances, why didn't you come and sit with us where we always sit?' You didn't say anything to me, and it made me very angry. I knew you had told me earlier that your father wasn't driving you to the ballgame. I couldn't understand how my best friend could come to the game and wouldn't sit with me; and when I see you in the bathroom mirror, you won't talk to me. So, I said, 'Carrie Frances, why won't you speak to me? Did I do anything wrong to you?' You turned around and said, 'I don't know you and my name is not Carrie Frances!' I said, 'Yes, you are Carrie Frances, we go to school together and we are in the sixth grade.' She told me her name and that she went to school in Lenheim, which is about five miles away. I looked at the outfit she was wearing and realized that you didn't have anything like that in your closet, because you and I know what kind of clothes each of us has. I told her that she looked just like your twin and I apologized to her for being angry at her. I also told her that I couldn't wait for the next day to come so I could tell my best friend that she has a twin lookalike living only five miles away." (End of 1 Encounter)

2 ENCOUNTER:

My father's niece, Nuntsy, has a son, Henry Lee (Buddy), who joined the Peace Corps when I was in the tenth grade. We were very good friends as well as cousins. He would write me letters and send me pictures of him and places that he visited. I was always so happy to hear from him.

They lived right across the field and road from us. One day my mother went to visit Nuntsy and she told Momma that she had received a letter from Buddy.

And Buddy told her to tell me that he got married and his wife looks exactly like me and has my same name, Carrie Frances, and now that they are married, she has my full name being that Buddy and I share the same last name. He also said he was going to send a picture so I could see that we looked like Identical twins. (End of 2 Encounter)

3 ENCOUNTER:

After graduating from high school and living in New York, one morning I had a phone call, and to my surprise it was the telephone operator; with an unusual request from a Carrie Frances with my same last name from Kansas City, Missouri. She was looking for a friend with the same name who lived in Brooklyn, New York, but the phone number was disconnected.

She pleaded with the operator to give her a listing for someone with the same name in case it was her friend. The operator told her there was only one listing with that name and it was unlisted. The operator called my number and explained the situation and asked if I would agree to talk to this person.

Being that the name was the same as my cousin Buddy's wife and from Kansas City, Missouri, I agreed to accept the call. I thought it might be Buddy's wife calling with information about him, but it wasn't. I looked in the phone book and sure enough there was a listing of someone living not too far from me with the same name.

After talking to the other Carrie Frances on the phone, she said she was not married to my cousin,

Buddy. Instead, she was trying to contact her best friend that she had met while dancing in Missouri. They had become great friends because they had the same full name and looked like identical twins. I agreed to go to the address and see if I could give the person the message from her friend from Missouri. Sure enough, the name was on the mailbox on the porch, but no one answered. I could tell that someone was watching from inside of the hallway, but very quietly. I left a note explaining everything and the information from the girl in Missouri. (End of 3 Encounter)

4 Encounter:

About a year or so later, my god brother, David was at a night club watching a striptease; the female dancer was doing a tease that was so distasteful that he went on stage, dragged her off, and began to beat her because he thought it was me.

He couldn't believe that his god sister would be on stage doing something so DISTASTEFUL that even the men in the audience couldn't take it. He thought it was me because she looked identical to me and her name was the same as mine. The full name.

She pleaded so badly telling him that she didn't know him, until he called me while holding her down with the other hand. When I answered the phone, he asked, "Is that you, Carrie Frances?" I said, "Yes it's me." He then explained what was happening. He told me, "You have a twin lookalike with your full name. And you better be careful because this girl is doing things that will give you a bad name because she looks identical to you and has your same full name." He let the girl loose and apologized immediately and went on about his business. (End of 4 Encounter)

5 Encounter:

Some years later my boyfriend called me and asked, "Are you home?" I replied, "Of course I'm home; how else would you be talking to me?" He went on to say, "I just ran up behind you and kissed you on the cheek and you slapped me; that's why I called to see if you were home or if it was you pretending that it wasn't you. The woman looked identical to you in every way except for her outfit. She even has your same full name too." (End of 5 Encounter)

6 Encounter:

Years later my kids were on the train going to school and they saw me sitting across from them and started saying, "Hi Momma, where are you going?" The woman said, "I am not your mother. I don't have any kids." My kids went on to tell the woman that she was their mother and her name was Carrie Frances. The woman told them her full name, including the last name, and it was exactly as mine. After a while my kids realized that I didn't have any clothes in my closet like the ones the woman was wearing.

A short time later one of my kids saw the same woman a second time. (End of 6 Encounter)

7 ENCOUNTER:

About a year later, my godmother was on the subway and saw me and started a conversation and the lookalike twin told her, "I don't know you, miss." My godmother said, "Carrie Frances, why are you fooling around with your poor old momma?" The woman said, "Miss, I am serious, I don't know you, but my name is Carrie Frances."

It turns out that this woman was my identical twin and had my full name as well. Momma went on and very proudly told the woman all about me and my work at the studios, theatre and film work. The woman went on to say, "I wish I did have a life like that." (End of 7 Encounter)

8 ENCOUNTER:

A few months later while working at DEF Studio in Manhattan, New York, the identical twin lookalike was there as an extra, dressed in the exact same coat and scarf as mine. And what's so ironic is that her hair was in a braided style exactly as mine. I said to myself, "This woman has been watching me."

I wasn't supposed to touch up the extras, but that day after I touched up my main talent, I went over to her and she ran from me. I called her back and told her I had to check out her hair so I could get a good look at her face. She kept fidgeting, trying not to let me see her face and to get away from me as fast as she could.

Later on, that day, I went to the studio cafeteria to see if I could talk to her. She was sitting at a table with her back to me talking to the other extras and one of the extras pointed out to her that I was at the door. She immediately held her head down on the table and pretended to be sleeping. (End of 8 Encounter)

9 ENCOUNTER:

In 1997, while working in Arizona on a film, I noticed that two Native American (Apache) women were staring at me. I immediately asked them what was wrong, and they said, "Nothing, but you look identical to a lady on our reservation." I asked, "What's her name?" They replied, "She goes by several different names and she comes and goes from the reservation. Sometimes she stays away from the reservation for years and then, sometimes she returns after a short time."

They invited me to visit them on the reservation. I happily accepted their invitation. As a matter of fact, it was an HONOR to go up to the Apache reservation on Whiteriver Mountain in Whiteriver, Arizona.

A few months later in November of 1997, while working on another film, we had a month hiatus. I went up to the Apache reservation on Whiteriver Mountain to visit them. I ran into all of the extras who were in the film and it was hundreds of them. I had a really great time.

I spent two weeks up there with them. A day or two before I left, I inquired about the identical twin lookalike, and the younger of the two women who invited me to visit took me to the arts and crafts center where she was supposed to be. I was told that she did a lot of sewing. The lady told me to wait in the car and she would go in and get her and make our introduction to each other.

Have you ever felt that someone was watching you? Well, on that day, I knew someone was watching me from inside of the center from the window. Shortly afterward, the lady came out of the building and by her walk and look on her face, I knew this identical twin lookalike was not coming out.

When the lady got back into the car, she said in an embarrassed, low tone, "She's not here!" I said to her, "I know she's in there, but she doesn't want to come out. She was watching me from the window. I felt it. Also, I am positive that our paths have crossed more than one time and she doesn't want me to see her in her hideout safe haven place." We left and no more was said about it. (End of 9 Encounter)

"That was my last encounter with my identical twin lookalike."

Viola is almost speechless and at the same time holding her hands over her mouth to keep from laughing. Then she says, "Oh my God! It all started from that night at the ball game when we were in the sixth grade." Carrie Frances says, "Yes, it did but I never thought it would be that many encounters. I truly believe it was the same person except the girl that my cousin Buddy married. I think the girl in the bathroom is the real culprit and planned everything out from that night and started using my name." Viola says, "Carrie Frances, I am so happy that you told me this and in private too. It goes to show you that people start scheming at a very young age and you also have to be extremely careful." Carrie Frances shakes her head and says softly, "Yes, that is so true."

Bible Thief

Viola looks around and notices some Bibles stacked on a small table near the window and asks, "Carrie Frances! What are you doing with all of those Bibles? Where did you get them?" Carrie Frances's mind is really on something else now. She looks at the Bibles, looks at Viola, smiles, and in a soft voice, she says, "I stole them." Viola laughs in disbelief and says, "No, you didn't." Carrie Frances, with a serious look, replies, "Yes, I did." Viola asks, "How and why?" Carrie Frances tells her, "Well, many years ago I took them from different hotels."

Viola looks confused and says, "Carrie Frances, I am waiting on this story too." She sits up straight and says, "Go on, tell me." Carrie Frances props herself up in bed with pillows. She tells Viola the story, but she doesn't tell the whole truth. As a matter of fact, while she is telling the BS story, she's actually visualizing the true story as it happened. Carrie Frances, with a straight face, says, "All right, here it goes."

Flashback-1973 New York City-
The Real Story-Statler Hilton Hotel

A room service table with food is all set up. Carrie Frances is lying in bed looking bored. She turns the television on and turns the channels. She is still bored. She looks at her watch and glances over at the dresser. She is so bored that she looks in the desk drawer by the bed not expecting to find anything. To her surprise she sees a Bible. She can't believe it; she's excited to see the Bible. Immediately, she flips through the Bible and reads. She holds the Bible to her chest with excitement and gets up and puts the Bible in her pocketbook.

A knock is heard at the door and she answers it. An Italian man comes in and kisses her. They sit down at the table and have dinner.

Statler Hilton Hotel-Different Room-Another Day

A room service table with food is set up. Carrie Frances is sitting in a chair in a different hotel room.

She is bored again and opens the desk drawer and sees a Bible. Carrie Frances is excited again and goes through the same routine again and puts the Bible in her pocketbook.

A knock is heard at the door. She opens the door and invites the man in. It's a different man this time. This man is Jewish with a briefcase. He kisses her also. Once again, Carrie Frances and the man sit at the table and have dinner.

Statler Hilton Hotel-Different Room-Another Day

Carrie Frances is in a different hotel room. She is bored beyond bored. She looks in the desk drawer and sees another Bible again. This time she's confused. She takes the Bible and puts it in her pocketbook. A knock is heard at the door. She answers the door and it's the same Italian man from before. Carrie Frances and the man kiss. They sit at the table to have dinner. Carrie Frances says to her boyfriend, "Garry, I found a Bible in the desk drawer. I guess somebody left it by mistake."

Garry laughs and says, "No, darling, all hotels have Bibles in their rooms."

Carrie Frances, surprised, says, "I didn't know that." She looks at Garry and says, "Well, I am taking this one home, because I don't have a Bible." He replies with a sweet smile and says, "I'll buy you one." Carrie Frances says, "Thanks, but I'll buy one soon."

Abraham and Strauss-December-1973

Carrie Frances is looking at Bibles in the stationery department. She picks out a large Saint James Bible and smiles and goes to the checkout counter.

Carrie Frances's Apartment-1973

A few days later Carrie Frances is sitting in her living room with a neighbor, talking. She has her newly bought Bible on the coffee table. The female neighbor, looking at the Bible, says, "Carrie Frances, I see you have a Bible. That's nice. I don't have one. I need to get one." Carrie Frances is happy to hear that and smiles and says, "Oh, I have an extra one. You can have it." She gets up and goes to the hallway closet and comes back with one of the Bibles that she took from the hotel. She gives the Bible to the neighbor and says, "Here, you can have this one." The neighbor is so happy and says, "Thank you so much." She takes the Bible and holds it to her chest. Carrie Frances, smiling says, "You are more than welcome."

(End of Bible Thief Flashback)

Carrie Frances, lying, says, "You see, Viola, my job took me to different places, so I had to stay in different hotels. I would get bored with nothing to do after work sometimes. One night I started looking through the hotel desk drawer and I found a Bible. I thought someone had left it by mistake. I was surprised and happy, so I read the Bible. Being that I didn't have one at home, I decided to take it. I knew the Lord would not hold it against me because it was the good book." She looks at Viola and says, "So, after that, I always checked the desk drawers in hotels to see if someone had forgotten their Bible. Sure enough, I continued to find Bibles and I took them all home. It took a while for me to realize that all hotels had Bibles in their rooms. I found that out from my girlfriend. I ended up buying a Bible as a Christmas gift for myself. Viola, that was the best gift that I ever bought for myself and it meant more to me than any gift I ever received from anyone else. I was so happy to have my own family Bible. I gave my friends most of the Bibles that I stole from the hotels. And believe it or not, they were happy to get a Bible, because they didn't have one." She looks at Viola again and says, "I truly believe the Lord intended for me to take those Bibles so I could pass them along to people who didn't have one. You know, not everybody would steal a Bible, but the Lord knew I would. I believe that's why he put me in the right place at the right time."

Viola is on the floor laughing. Maggie Mae and Caleb hear the laughter and come into the bedroom. Maggie Mae, excited says, "Whut's going on?" Caleb asks, "Whuts y'all laufin' 'bout?" Viola gets up off the floor and says, "Carrie Frances told me a story about the Bibles." She points to the Bibles and continues,

"Look, see all of those Bibles. She stole them." Viola bursts out laughing. Caleb asks, "Cusin Ker Francie, you sol a Bible?" Carrie Frances, laughing, says, "Yes, I did." Viola, laughing, tries to tell the story, saying, "She stole them from different hotels that she was staying in, while working in different places, and she gave them to her friends that didn't have a Bible." Maggie Mae says, "Well, I could use one. Give me one." Caleb says, "Gimme one too, cusin Ker Frances." Viola, laughing, says, "I'll take one too."

Carrie Frances, laughing, says, "I don't see why not. Take them. That's why I stole them in the first place, to give to people who wanted one."

Maggie Mae, Caleb, and Viola take the last three stolen Bibles from Carrie Frances.

The Funeral

Carrie Frances, Maggie Mae, and Cousin Caleb drive up to the church. Everybody from Silo and all of the nearby towns are there. Carrie Frances realizes what Maggie Mae said was true. She has been away for so long that she has forgotten how Southern folks enjoy going to funerals and she says, "God! Everybody is here, look, there's Tuck. Oh my god, I know that guy's face, but I can't remember his name." Maggie Mae happily says, "I told you, you'd see everybody here."

They all get out of the car. On the way into the church they have conversations with different people. Carrie Frances is looking gorgeous. The men are having a field day eyeing her.

The church is filled to capacity. It's standing room

only. Carrie Frances sees one seat available at the back of the church. Caleb proudly escorts her to the seat. One of the ushers finds a seat for Maggie Mae. Caleb stands near Cousin Carrie Frances where she is sitting in the rear of the church. All eyes are on Carrie Frances; some happy smiles and some eyes with envy. Carrie Frances sees a childhood friend that she recognizes from grade school. They smile at each other with tears in their eyes.

The family procession comes in. Sure enough, Ola Jean is wearing a beautiful white mink hat, and Loletha is sporting a new weave; both are all dressed in white, crying uncontrollably, and falling all over the place.

Carrie Frances thinks, *Oh, god! Viola was right. They do carry on.*

Carrie Frances finds herself crying. An usher comes along and hands her a tissue.

As the family walks out of the church, Ola Jean, Loletha, and a cousin falls onto the floor and have to be carried out of the church. As Carrie Frances walks out of the church, she gets weak and Cousin Caleb has to help her. While going down the steps she sees a boyfriend from high school that she has not seen since she was fourteen years old and he was fifteen years old.

Suddenly, while Carrie Frances is being helped down the steps by Cousin Caleb, a pall bearer extends his hand to help her also and says, "Hi Caleb." Cousin Caleb replies, "Hi, Charlie Jay." Carrie Frances whispers to Cousin Caleb and says, "Caleb, Charlie Jay doesn't know who I am." Cousin Caleb says, "I know, go back and tell him who you are." Carrie Frances takes Cousin

Caleb's advice because that was one of her favorite loves in junior high school. She walks back to Charlie Jay and says softly, "Charlie Jay, you don't know who I am, do you?" He replies slowly, "No." She answers, "I am Carrie Frances." Charlie Jay, excited and smiling, says, "Girl, you look good. When I reached for your hand coming down the steps, I said to myself, 'that's a good-looking woman.'"

Charlie Jay hugs Carrie Frances and they continue talking. He asks her, "Where do you live?" She tells him, "I live in New York, but my house here is in Dranchwood on Highway 8." He replies with a sweet smile, "I am going to stop by, all right?" She gives him a big smile and says, "Okay, see you later." Cousin Caleb is looking on as if he has done something great. It makes Carrie Frances think of what Maggie Mae had said, "You might meet a man."

Carrie Frances continues talking to other people. It's like a family and class reunion. Carrie Frances sees her oldest sister's best friend. She hasn't seen her since she was three years old, but she recognizes her. The lady is shocked and happy that Carrie Frances remembers her. Everybody is having such a good time that it takes a while to leave.

Shears Church Cemetery

People are walking around talking to each other. The family comes and sits by the grave site. Carrie Frances is still talking to people she has not seen in over twenty-eight years. She watches the ceremony with sadness. She is almost in a daze, not really believing that Billy C is gone. The family leaves the grave site.

Carrie Frances stops talking to people and glances at Billy C's coffin being put in the ground. She watches Billy C being covered up and she says in her mind, I love you. She walks on slowly, leaving the cemetery, and sees a cousin and kisses him.

She gets into the car with Maggie Mae and Cousin Caleb and drives off.

Happy New Year

The family goes back to Ola Jean and Loletha's house. Most of them are sitting around eating and talking. Someone calls on the telephone and asks to speak to Ola Jean or Loletha. Ola Jean goes to the phone. The person says, "There's a surprise for you and Loletha on the front porch. Don't tell anyone. Go and get it before some of your guests see it." The person hangs up the phone. Ola Jean is half scared and happy at the same time. She and Loletha go onto the front porch and see a beautiful Christmas shopping bag with two beautifully wrapped gifts in it. One of the gifts has Ola Jean's name on it; The other gift has Loletha's name on it. They each open their gift on the porch, and they see the money; they look at each other and run back into the house.

A few days later, Carrie Frances, Viola, Maggie Mae, Cousin Caleb, and, believe it or not, Benjy the police officer are all sitting together in the movie theater. Their eyes are on the screen as the credits roll. Carrie Frances is pointing at the screen, showing them her name. They all look on with joy and happy smiles on their faces. The End

EPILOGUE

Immediately after Carrie Frances arrived back home in New York City from her traumatized holiday vacation, it was back to the old drawing board. It was so hard for her to wrap her head around what had just happened; some HORRIFIC and some extremely fantastic things occurred on her vacation. The pain from the loss of her beloved Billy C was almost unbearable, but on the other hand, there was the joy and gratification that she got when that old lady got the best New Year's gift ever. JUSTICE will forever be a bright beacon of light shining in her heart!

A day or so later, Carrie Frances was back to work on the set as usual, trying to make the best of everything. Suddenly, a coworker informed her of a special news bulletin. She listened to what was being said in shock. The date was January 8, 2003. After hearing the news bulletin, Carrie Frances was very happy that she heard, listened and obeyed that soft voice that said,

"WATCH OUT FOR YOUR LUGGAGE!"

After a couple of years went by Carrie Frances was back to her old normal self, while occasionally thinking of her past trials and tribulations. While working one day, she had an encounter that she had never experienced in her life. Have you ever thought you had felt something a couple of times in your life and realized in an instant that you had not and that this was the first experience of such a feeling? Well, this is what happened to Carrie Frances. Being a Christian, when things happen such as this, you have to leave it in God's hands. The only thing Carrie Frances could do was acknowledge God's presence and say, *"Oh my God, so this is who you have been saving me for all of my life, this young man. Well, so be it!"* It was as if GOD had opened up the GATES OF HEAVEN WITH EVERLASTING LOVE, HAPPINESS, JOY, PEACE AND CONTENTMENT in an instant. What she learned from this experience and encounter was that you must pray, put God first, and wait on the Lord for guidance and the answers to everything on your journey in life.

Many years have come and gone now, and Carrie Frances is still happy and enjoying life to the fullest. But one thing weighs on her mind and heart very heavily: her SLAVE ANCESTORS! She has always thought of them from childhood, while listening to the stories that her parents, older relatives, and friends would tell at gatherings. Now that she is older, it's as if it's her duty to seek justice for them. As a matter of fact, she feels compelled to do so.

Growing up in the Jim Crow South era, as a small

child, she saw the hardships that so many people went through. Families having to sneak and move away in the middle of night because the landowner wouldn't let them move because he said they owed him money for the past fifteen to twenty years. However, this wasn't true because the sharecropper families knew they didn't owe any money to the owner of the land; but because they couldn't keep their own books about what was made on the farm, there was nothing they could do except stay and continue being cheated by the owner until they couldn't take it anymore. THIS WAS ANOTHER FORM OF SLAVERY—free but not free!

Some children of sharecroppers had to start work in the fields as young as five years old. When school started, they could only go on rainy days when they couldn't work the fields. Those children were given the name "RAIN CHILDREN." <u>Also, the school year, summer school, began June 15 and went through the end of July. School started up again in the fall on October 15 and ended the last of May or the 1st of June, which enabled the children to work the fields up until October 15 or until the cotton was finished; sometimes the cotton wasn't finished until late December.</u> Now, here is the kicker: during summer school the older children had to work in tobacco, and therefore, they couldn't attend school unless it rained. Many children quit school because they were ashamed that they could only go to school on rainy days and it was so hard to catch up with their lessons; and besides, some children who were fortunate enough not to have to work on the farms would laugh and make jokes about them.

This type of farm work for sharecroppers and their families went on beyond the Civil Rights Act of 1964. As a matter of fact, it went on until the mid-1970s'.

Having said all of the above, it's nothing compared to what our slave ancestors went through.

They were slaves for over two centuries; (1619-1865), 246 years of slavery. <u>They worked from sunup to sundown, barely clothed and with bare feet. The food they were fed were the scraps from the master's house and some of them were fed out of a hog trough. They were beaten, hanged, and some thrown into scalding hot water alive. Male and female slaves were raped by the slave masters, forced breeding, whipped into oblivion, families separated and sold, even newborn babies. They weren't allowed to read and write, and if any slaves were caught doing such, they would be punished by cutting a limb off or even being killed; it didn't matter money-wise because the slaves were insured as livestock.</u>

Abe Lincoln promised each slave forty acres and a mule as compensation for the harsh and inhumane treatment that they had endured. By doing this the freed slaves would be able to sustain themselves and have something to pass down the generations to their descendants.

By today's standards it would be forty acres and a tractor (not a mule); included with pain and suffering through the Jim Crow era, with added interest and today's money value for the past 154 years since the abolishing of slavery. The American government should have paid it immediately after abolishing slavery or at least in 1964 during the Civil Rights Act, but instead they decided to kick the can down the road to a later date and it is now 2019. What they owe the descendants of American slaves is over seven trillion dollars.

Anytime the topic of monetary reparation comes up, everyone angrily says, <u>"Oh, we can't do that."</u> While in the same breath they are spending trillions of dollars on unnecessary wars in other countries, building up other countries, giving money to every country on this earth, and one country in particular is given 36 billion annually in quarterly payments.

The government brings <u>refugees</u> to this country and gives them free benefits and legal immigrants (<u>without merit</u>) get free benefits also. **<u>Now, here's what's so ironic: Illegal aliens invade our country, the USA, on their own by choice; they demand that the USA take care of them and their children.</u>** <u>The USA government gives them FREE BENEFITS too!</u>

ILLEGAL ALIENS didn't come to the USA by FORCE in CHAINS AND SHACKLES as the AMERICAN SLAVES did.

Please understand this, if the USA government did not give money and benefits to the above mentioned countries, and individuals/groups of people, I would still feel the same way as I do about justice for the American slaves and their descendants, which is, PAY MONETARY REPARATIONS IN THE FORM OF A CHECK to the descendants of American slaves.

The USA government refuses to take care of its own; it refuses to **CORRECT the WRONGS** of the past.

In other words, **RIGHT the WRONGS** of what was done to the AMERICAN SLAVES and pay MONETARY REPARATIONS in the form of a CHECK to their DESCENDANTS.

*It is the moral thing to do and JUSTICE FOR THE AMERICAN SLAVES. *

In my opinion, anyone, regardless of color, who says and believes that the descendants of American slavery don't deserve and should not be paid MONETARY REPARATION in the form of a CHECK is a RACIST.

These same people who don't believe in monetary reparations for the descendants of American slavery agree with and rally for taking care of REFUGEES, LEGAL IMMIGRANTS (without MERIT) and ILLEGAL ALIENS. If that's not racist, then I don't know what is.

Now, let me be clear, even though I voice my opinion about what I know is the right thing to do, whether it hurts someone's feelings or not, I LOVE MY COUNTRY, the UNITED STATES OF AMERICA! It's just that most of the people in government office are not doing what they are supposed to do for the citizens of this country, especially for the people who built this country with their free slave labor.

The American slaves didn't get paid anything, not even one cent for the nearly two and a half centuries of work that they did here in AMERICA; 246 years (1619-1865).

The souls of AMERICAN SLAVES will not rest and have peace until their descendants get JUSTICE FOR THEM.

Carrie Frances is on a MISSION TO GET JUSTICE

FOR HER AMERICAN SLAVE ANCESTORS!

She is PRAYING, putting GOD first, and leaving everything in the LORD'S HANDS. You can't go wrong with GOD ON YOU SIDE!

"MAY GOD'S UNMEASURABLE BLESSINGS BE UPON YOU ALL."

www.ingramcontent.com/pod-product-compliance
Lightning Source LLC
Chambersburg PA
CBHW061452300426
44114CB00014B/1952